STUDENT BOOK

WorldView 1

MICHAEL ROST

Simon le Maistre   **Carina Lewis**   **Kevin Sharpe**

Simon Greenall
Series Editor, British English edition

Longman

WorldView Student Book 1

Authorized adaptation from the United Kingdom edition entitled *Language to Go*, First Edition, published by Pearson Education Limited publishing under its Longman imprint.
Copyright © 2002 by Pearson Education Limited

American English adaptation published by Pearson Education, Inc. Copyright © 2005.

Pearson Education, 10 Bank Street, White Plains, NY 10606

Editorial director: Pamela Fishman
Project manager: Irene Frankel
Senior development editor: Maretta Callahan
Vice president, director of design and production: Rhea Banker
Executive managing editor: Linda Moser
Associate managing editor: Mike Kemper
Art director: Elizabeth Carlson
Vice president, director of international marketing: Bruno Paul
Senior manufacturing buyer: Edie Pullman
Text and cover design: Elizabeth Carlson
Photo research: Aerin Csigay
Text composition: Word and Image Design
Text font: 10.5/13pt Utopia and 10/12pt Frutiger Bold

ISBN: 0-13-183995-0

Library of Congress Control Number: 2003115897

Printed in the United States of America
3 4 5 6 7 8 9 10–BAM–09 08 07 06 05

Text Credits
Page 21, *Hello, Goodbye.* Words and music by John Lennon and Paul McCartney. Copyright © 1967 Sony/ATV Songs LLC. Copyright renewed. All rights administered by Sony/ATV Music Publishing, 8 Music Square West, Nashville, TN 37203. International copyright secured. All rights reserved; 59 *Up on the Roof.* Words and music by Gerry Goffin and Carole King. © 1962 (Renewed 1990) Screen Gems-EMI Music Inc. All rights reserved. International copyright secured. Used by permission. 97 *Tom's Diner.* Words and music by Suzanne Vega. © 1987 WB Music Corp. and Waifersongs Ltd. All rights administered by WB Music Corp. All rights reserved. Used by permission of Warner Bros. Publications. 135 *Oh, Pretty Woman.* Words and music by Roy Orbison and Bill Dees. Copyright © 1964 Sony/ATV Songs LLC, Barbara Orbison Music Company, Orbi-Lee Music and R-Key Darkus Music. Copyright Renewed. All rights on behalf of Sony/ATV Songs LLC administered by Sony/ATV Music Publishing, 8 Music Square West, Nashville, TN 37203. All rights on behalf of Barbara Orbison Music Company, Orbi-Lee Music and R-Key Darkus Music administered by ICG. International copyright secured. All rights reserved.

Illustration Credits
CrowleArt Group, p. 10; Paul McCusker, pp. 9, 33, 85, 94, 132; Suzanne Mogensen, pp. 77, 140; NSV Productions, pp. 102, 104, 105, 112, 114, 139; Steve Schulman, pp. 54, 57, 58.

Photo Credits
Page 2 *(left)* Jack Hollingsworth/Corbis, *(right)* Michal Heron; 3 Jules Perrier/Corbis; 4 Telegraph Colour Library; 5 Gilbert Duclos; 6 *(A)* DiMaggio/Kalish/Corbis, *(B)* Chris Ryan/Getty Images, *(C)* Dave G. Houser/Corbis, *(D)* Gabe Palmer/Corbis, *(E)* Michael Newman/PhotoEdit, *(F)* David Young-Wolff/PhotoEdit, *(G)* Photomondo/Getty Images, *(H)* Doug Menuez/Getty Images; 7 *(I)* Alvis Upitis/Getty Images, *(J)* Jose Luis Pelaez, Inc./Corbis, *(K)* Alan Carey/The Image Works, *(L)* Jose Luis Pelaez, Inc./Corbis; 8 Alvis Upitis/Getty Images; 11 *(top)* Corbis, *(middle left)* Anthony Blake Photo Library, *(middle right)* Corbis, *(bottom right)* Popperfoto; 13 Corbis; 14 *(top)* C Squared Studios/Getty Images, *(middle)* Bill Aron/PhotoEdit, *(bottom)* Getty Images; 15 *(top left)* C Squared Studios/Getty Images, *(top right)* Trevor Clifford, *(middle left)* David Young-Wolff/PhotoEdit, *(middle)* Park Street/PhotoEdit, *(middle right)* Royalty-Free/Corbis, *(bottom left)* Siede Preis/Getty Images, *(bottom middle)* Siede Preis/Getty Images, *(bottom right)* Amy Etra/PhotoEdit; 16 Kim Kulish/Corbis SABA; 18 *(left)* Jack Hollingsworth/Corbis, *(right)* Jules Perrier/Corbis; 19 *(judo)* TRBfoto/Getty Images, *(baseball)* Mark Scott/Getty Images, *(Williams)* AFP/Corbis, *(Iglesais)* AFP/Corbis, *(flamenco)* Pete Saloutos/Corbis, *(origami)* Steve Cole/Getty Images, *(Bundchen)* Popperfoto, *(souvlaki)* Brian Hagiwara/Foodpix, *(burritos)* Ann Stratton/Foodpix, *(pizza)* Royalty-Free/Corbis, *(sushi)* Corbis; 20 Bettmann/Corbis; 22 *(left)* Corbis, *(top right)* Gareth Bowden, *(bottom right)* Trevor Clifford; 23 *(top left)* Image State, *(bottom left)* Daniel Bosler/Getty Images, *(top right)* Pictor International, *(top right middle)* Getty Images, *(bottom right middle)* Greg Evans Picture Library, *(bottom right)* Image State; 24 Getty Images; 27 *(left)* Retna, *(right)* Powerstock Zefa; 28 Romilly Lockyer /Getty Images; 31 Rex Features; 34 *(left)* Getty Images, *(top right)* Aspect Picture Library, *(bottom right)* Impact Photos; 35 Aspect Picture Library; 36 Akira Nakata/HAGA/The Image Works; 38 Anthony Blake Photo Library; 39 William McKellar/Brand X Pictures/PictureQuest; 40 Rex Features; 46 David Young-Wolff/PhotoEdit; 48 Trevor Clifford; 50 *(top)* Kim Heacox/Getty Images, *(bottom)* Vera Storman/Getty Images; 51 *(left)* ML Sinibaldi/Corbis, *(right)* Image State; 53 Greg Pease/Getty Images; 55 *(shirt)* Royalty-Free/Corbis, *(shorts)* David Young-Wolff/PhotoEdit, *(sneakers)* Spencer Grant/PhotoEdit, *(suit)* Gareth Bowden, *(shirt)* Steve Gorton/Dorling Kindersley Media Library, *(sweater)* David Young-Wolff/PhotoEdit, *(coat)* Dorling Kindersley Media Library, *(pants)* David Young-Wolff/PhotoEdit, *(skirt)* Steve Gorton/Dorling Kindersley Media Library; 56 *(books)* Stephen Oliver/Dorling Kindersley Media Library, *(poster)* Swim Ink/Corbis, *(CDs)* Keith Brofsky/Getty Images, *(watches)* Paul Bricknell/Dorling Kindersley Media Library, *(videos)* Royalty-Free/Corbis, *(plates)* Peter Harholdt/Corbis, *(car)* Tim Ridley/Dorling Kindersley Media Library, *(doll)* Dorling Kindersley Media Library, *(photos)* Bob Krist/Corbis, *(cards)* Guy Motil/Corbis, *(clock)* Paul Bricknell/ Dorling Kindersley Media Library; 58 Hulton Archive/Getty Images; 60 *(A)* Rita Maas/Getty Images, *(B)* John William Banagan/Getty Images, *(C)* Lars Klove/Getty Images, *(D)* David Young-Wolff/PhotoEdit, *(E)* David Young-Wolff/PhotoEdit, *(F)* Tony Freeman/PhotoEdit, *(G)* C Squared Studios/Getty Images, *(H)* Felicia Martinez/PhotoEdit, *(I)* Mitch Hrdlicka/Getty Images, *(J)* Chris Collins/Corbis, *(K)* C Squared Studios/Getty Images, *(L)* Felicia Martinez/PhotoEdit, *(M)* Royalty-Free/Corbis, *(N)* Christel Rosenfeld/Getty Images, *(O)* C Squared Studios/Photodisc/PictureQuest; 64 David Young-Wolff/PhotoEdit; 65 Image State; 66 Richard Price/Getty Images; 74 Getty Imges; 78 Britstock-IFA; 80 Daniel Bosler/Getty Images; 82 *(top left)* Hulton Archive/Getty Images, *(top right)* Getty Images, *(bottom)* David Young-Wolff/Getty Images; 86 Robert Harding Picture Library; 87 Getty Images; 88 Robert Harding Picture Library; 93 Tim Pannell/Corbis; 96 Flusin Lionel/Corbis KIPA, *(A)* Randy Faris/Corbis, *(B)* James Leynse/Corbis SABA, *(C)* Ryan McVay/Getty Images, *(D)* Ed Taylor/Getty Images, *(E)* Peter Hvizdak/The Image Works, *(F)* Robert Holmes/Corbis; 98 Moviestore Collection; 99 Corbis; 100 Scott Harrison/Getty Images; 103 Bob Krist/Corbis; 106 *(left)* Trevor Clifford, *(inset)* Trevor Clifford; 107 Greg Evans Picture Library; 108 Tom & Dee Ann McCarthy/Corbis; 110 The Photographers Library; 111 Powerstock Zefa; 112 Steve Allen/Getty Images; 115 Tom & Dee Ann McCarthy/Corbis; 118 *(top)* K.K.Yu/Corbis, *(bottom)* Tony Hopewell/Getty Images; 120 *(top left)* Pictor International, *(bottom left)* Greg Evans Picture Library, *(top right)* Robert Harding Picture Library, *(bottom right)* Art Directors and Trip; 121 Getty Images; 124 *(top)* The Photographers Library, *(bottom left)* Corbis, *(bottom right)* Solo per Due; 131 *(top)* Powerstock Zefa, *(bottom)* Corbis; 133 The Photographers Library; 134 Corbis Bettmann.

Introduction

Welcome to *WorldView*, a four-level English course for adults and young adults. *WorldView* builds fluency by exploring a wide range of compelling topics presented from an international perspective. A trademark two-page lesson design, with clear and attainable language goals, ensures that students feel a sense of accomplishment and increased self-confidence in every class.

WorldView's approach to language learning follows a simple and proven **MAP**:
• **M**otivate learning through stimulating content and achievable learning goals.
• **A**nchor language production with strong, focused language presentations.
• **P**ersonalize learning through engaging and communicative speaking activities.

Course components

• **Student Book with Student Audio CD**
  The Student Book contains 28, four-page units; seven Review Units (one after every four units); four World of Music Units (two in each half of the book); Information for Pair and Group Work; a Vocabulary list; and a Grammar Reference section.

  The Student Audio CD includes tracks for all pronunciation and listening exercises (or reading texts, in selected units) in the *Student Book*. The Student Audio CD can be used with the *Student Book* for self-study and coordinates with the *Workbook* listening and pronunciation exercises.

• For each activity in the *Student Book*, the interleaved **Teacher's Edition** provides step-by-step procedures and exercise answer keys as well as a wealth of teacher support: unit Warm-ups, Optional Activities, Extensions, Culture Notes, Background Information, Teaching Tips, Wrap-ups, and extensive Language Notes. In addition, the *Teacher's Edition* includes a course orientation guide, full audio scripts, and the *Workbook* answer key.

• **The Workbook** has 28 three-page units that correspond to each of the *Student Book* units. Used in conjunction with the Student Audio CD, the *Workbook* provides abundant review and practice activities for Vocabulary, Grammar, Listening, and Pronunciation, along with Self-Quizzes after every four units. A Learning Strategies section at the beginning of the *Workbook* helps students to be active learners.

• **The Class Audio Program** is available in either CD or cassette format and contains all the recorded material for in-class use.

• **The Teacher's Resource Book** (with **Testing Audio CD** and **TestGen Software**) has three sections of reproducible material: extra communication activities for in-class use, model writing passages for each *Student Book* writing assignment, and a complete testing program: seven quizzes and two tests, along with scoring guides and answer keys. Also included are a Testing Audio CD for use with the quizzes and tests and an easy-to-use TestGen software CD for customizing the tests.

• For each level of the course, the ***WorldView* Video** presents seven, five-minute authentic video segments connected to *Student Book* topics. Notes to the Teacher are available in the Video package, and Student Activity Sheets can be downloaded from the ***WorldView* Companion Website**.

• The *WorldView* **Companion Website** (www.longman.com/worldview) provides a variety of teaching support, including Video Activity Sheets and supplemental reading material.

Unit contents

Each of the 28 units in *WorldView* has seven closely linked sections:
• **Getting started:** a communicative opening exercise that introduces target vocabulary
• **Listening/Reading:** a functional conversation or thematic passage that introduces target grammar
• **Grammar focus:** an exercise sequence that allows students to focus on the new grammar point and to solidify their learning
• **Pronunciation:** stress, rhythm, and intonation practice based on the target vocabulary and grammar
• **Speaking:** an interactive speaking task focused on student production of target vocabulary, grammar, and functional language
• **Writing:** a personalized writing activity that stimulates student production of target vocabulary and grammar
• **Conversation to go:** a concise reminder of the grammar functional language introduced in the unit

Course length

With its flexible format and course components, *WorldView* responds to a variety of course needs, and is suitable for 70 to 90 hours of classroom instruction. Each unit can be easily expanded by using bonus activities from the *Teacher's Edition*, reproducible activities available in the *Teacher's Resource Book*, linked lessons from the *WorldView* Video program, and supplementary reading assignments in the *WorldView* Companion Website.

The *WorldView Student Book* with Student Audio CD and the *Workbook* are also available in split editions.

Scope and Sequence

GRAMMAR FOCUS	PRONUNCIATION	SPEAKING	WRITING
be simple present: affirmative statements, subject pronouns	Sentence rhythm	Saying *hello* and *goodbye*; introducing yourself; spelling names	Write people's names correctly
be simple present: *am, is, are*; subject pronouns; Indefinite articles: *a, an*	Contractions with *be*	Making introductions	Describe two friends and their occupations
be simple present: *Yes/No* questions, short answers and negative statements	Rising intonation for *Yes/No* questions	Asking about nationalities	Write an international quiz
Plurals; *be* simple present: *Wh–* questions	Falling intonation for *wh–* questions and statements	Asking for and giving information	Write information on order form for office supplies
Possessive adjectives and Possessive *'s*	Weak forms: possessive adjectives	Talking about people and favorite things	Write a paragraph about a friend's favorite things
There is/There are	The voiced *th* sound /ð/ in *there*	Talking about places you know	Write a review of your favorite place in a city or town
Prepositions of location	Stress in words	Telling someone where things are in a room	Describe an office or living room
Simple present: affirmative statements	3rd person -*s*/-*es* ending	Talking about holidays	Write a letter to a friend about a special day or a holiday
Simple present: *Yes/No* questions, short answers negative statements	Stressed and weak syllables in words	Talking about possessions	Write a paragraph collectibles or a collection in a museum
Simple present: *Wh–* questions	Weak forms: *do/does* in questions	Talking about ways of communicating	Describe how you communicate in a typical week
A, an, some, any	Weak forms: *a, an, some, any*	Talking about vacations	Describe your travel plans, including things to pack and how you will travel
Demonstrative adjectives: *this, that, these, those*	Focus words	Asking for information in a store	Make a shopping list of clothes you need, including items, colors, and sizes
Count and non-count nouns; *How much/How many*; Quantifiers: *much, many, a lot of*	Vowel sounds: /ɑ/ in *not* and /ʌ/ in *nut*	Talking about the foods you like	Write an email about foods you like and how much you eat
Modal: *can* for ability	Weak and strong forms: *can* and *can't*	Asking about job skills	Describe your job skills, including skills you want to learn

Lesson A

Here's my card.

Vocabulary Greetings and leave-takings; introductions; names; the alphabet
Grammar *be* simple present: affirmative statements; subject pronouns
Speaking Saying hello and goodbye; introducing yourself; spelling names

Listening

1 Look at photos A–C. What are the people doing? What are they saying?

2 🎧 Listen to three conversations. Which conversation matches each photo?

Photo A _____   Photo B _____   Photo C _____

3 *PAIRS.* Compare your answers.

4 🎧 Listen and complete the conversation between Grace Lee and Miguel Santos.

A: _____. _____ Grace Lee.

B: _____. _____ Miguel Santos.

A: _____ you.

B: _____ you, too.

A: _____ my business card. _____ the Valdez Group.

B: _____.

A: _____.

B: Goodbye.

5 *PAIRS.* Compare your answers.

2

Pronunciation

6 🎧 Listen. Notice the rhythm of the sentences. The important words are longer and stronger.

my **card**	**Here's** my **card**.
Hertz	**I'm** with **Hertz**.
meet you	**Pleased** to **meet** you.
you, too	**Nice** to meet **you**, **too**.
later	**See** you **lat**er.

7 🎧 Listen and repeat.

8 *PAIRS.* Practice the conversation in Exercise 4. Use your own names.

Speaking

9 *PAIRS.* Create a new conversation. Use your own names and the phrases and sentences in the box.

©

> Hello. / Hi!
> I'm . . . / My name is . . .
> Excuse me, what's your name again?
> Pleased to meet you. / Nice to meet you.
> Nice to meet you, too.
> Here's my card. I'm with . . .
> Thanks. / Thank you.
> Goodbye. / Bye! / See you. / So long!

10 *PAIRS.* Practice the new conversation.

Listening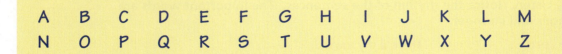

A	B	C	D	E	F	G	H	I	J	K	L	M
N	O	P	Q	R	S	T	U	V	W	X	Y	Z

1 🎧 Listen and repeat the letters of the alphabet.

2 🎧 Listen to the conversation and write the names you hear.

Name: _____ Company: _____ *Systems*

3 *PAIRS.* Take turns spelling your first and last names. Write your partner's name.

A: *Could you please spell your name?*
B: *Sure. My first name is . . .*

Grammar focus

4 Study the examples of the verb *be* with singular subjects in the simple present tense.

> **I'm** Miguel.   **My name is** Sarah Boyd.
> **Here's** my card.   **It's** nice meeting you.

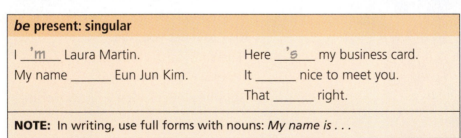

5 Look at the examples again. Complete the chart.

> ***be* present: singular**
>
> I __'m__ Laura Martin.   Here __'s__ my business card.
> My name _____ Eun Jun Kim.   It _____ nice to meet you.
>   That _____ right.
>
> **NOTE:** In writing, use full forms with nouns: *My name is . . .*

⊃ **Grammar Reference page 142**

6 Complete the sentences with the correct form of the verb *be*. Use contractions when possible.

1. A: Hi, I __'m__ Diego.

   B: Nice to meet you, Mr. Diego.

   A: Oh! Diego _____ my first name!

2. A: Hello. My name _____ Kelly.

   B: Kelly?

   A: That _____ right.

3. A: Nice to meet you.

   B: It _____ nice to meet you, too.

4. A: Hello, I _____ Paul Stamos.

   B: Hello. My name _____ Janet Gordon.

   Here _____ my card.

Writing

7 *PAIRS.* Student A, look at page 136. Student B, write the names you hear.

8 Switch roles. Student B, look at page 139. Student A, write the names you hear.

9 *PAIRS.* Check your answers. Look at pages 136 and 139.

Speaking

10 Walk around the room and talk to everyone. Use your actual business card or make one.

- Say hello.
- Say your name.
- Shake hands.
- Give out your business card.
- Say goodbye.

CONVERSATION TO GO

A: **Hi. I'm** Walter.
B: **Hello.** My name **is** Amanda.

UNIT 2

Meeting people

Vocabulary Occupations; numbers 0–19
Grammar *be* simple present: *am*, *is*, *are*; subject pronouns; indefinite articles: *a*, *an*
Speaking Making introductions

Lesson A

Getting started

1. **PAIRS.** Match the occupations with the photos.

an architect _F_	an artist ____	an assistant ____
a businesswoman ____	a cashier ____	a doctor ____
an engineer ____	a flight attendant ____	a graphic designer ____
a musician ____	a teacher ____	a waiter ____

2. 🎧 Listen and check your answers. Then listen and repeat.

6

I

J

K

L

3 🎧 **Listen to the numbers and repeat.**

0	1	2	3	4	5	6	7	8	9
10	11	12	13	14	15	16	17	18	19

4 🎧 **Listen and write the telephone and extension numbers you hear.**

1. _____   2. _____   3. _____

4. _____   5. _____   6. _____

Listening

5 🎧 **Listen and connect the name tags that match the three introductions you hear.**

Hello, I'm
Sonia Smith
Engineer

Hello, I'm
Christopher Boswell
_____

Hello, I'm
Jiro Nakamura
_____

Hello, I'm
Kwang-Min Kim
_____

Hello, I'm
Michele Amado
_____

Hello, I'm
Regina Rebello
_____

Hello, I'm
Christine Samples
_____

Hello, I'm
Mike Amaral
_____

Hello, I'm
Tao Chang
_____

6 🎧 **Listen again. Write the occupations under the names.**

Grammar focus

1 Study the examples of the verb *be* in the simple present tense.

I'**m** a doctor.	He'**s** an assistant manager.	They'**re** friends.
You'**re** an artist.	She'**s** a teacher.	We'**re** roommates.

2 Look at the examples again. Complete the chart with the full forms of the verb *be*.

be simple present			
I _____am_____		We	
You _____	a musician.	You _____	musicians.
He/She _____		They	

NOTE: Use full forms in formal writing. Use contractions in conversations and informal writing.

3 Look at the examples again. Complete the rules for indefinite articles in the chart.

Indefinite articles: *a, an*
Use _____ with singular nouns that begin with consonant sounds.
Use _____ with singular nouns that begin with vowel sounds.

Grammar Reference page 142

4 Complete the sentences with *a* or *an* and the correct form of the verb *be*. Use contractions when possible.

1. A: Hello. My name __is__ Enrique Sousa. I _____ _____ teacher in Argentina.

   B: Nice to meet you. I _____ Sherry Pace. And this _____ Penny Jones. We _____ teachers, too. But in New York City!

2. A: Excuse me. What's your name?

   B: I _____ Todd Danes.

   A: What do you do?

   B: I _____ _____ engineer in this department.

3. A: This _____ Tonia Michaels, and this _____ Sasha Rodriguez. They _____ graphic designers.

   B: Nice to meet you.

4. A: John . . . ?

   B: Yes, I _____ John Johannsen. And you _____ . . . ?

   A: I _____ Eric Ross. And this _____ Janet Jones. We _____ assistant managers.

5 🎧 Listen and check your answers.

Pronunciation

6 🎧 **Listen. Notice the pronunciation of the contractions and the way words are linked together.**

I'm	I'm a doctor.	You're	You're an artist.
He's	He's an architect.	She's	She's a teacher.
We're	We're roomates.	They're	They're engineers.

7 🎧 **Listen again and repeat.**

Speaking

8 *GROUPS OF 3.* **Role-play. You are someone else—someone famous. Write your new name and occupation on a piece of paper. Students A and B, give your papers to Student C. Student C, introduce Student A to Student B.**

C: Bill, this is Serena Williams. Serena, this is Bill Gates.
A: Nice to meet you.
B: Nice to meet you, too.
C: Serena is a tennis player.
B: A tennis player? Great.
C: Bill is a businessman.
A: A businessman? Interesting!

Ichiro Suzuki
Baseball player

Bill Gates
Businessman

Serena Williams
Tennis player

Jennifer Lopez
Singer

Writing

9 **Think of two friends. Write a short description of them. Use the simple present of the verb *be*.**

CONVERSATION TO GO

A: Hello. **I'm** Len Jones. **I'm a** new designer in your department.
B: Hi. Nice to meet you. My name **is** Tania Mitsuda.

Around the world

Vocabulary Nationalities and countries
Grammar *be* simple present: *Yes/No* questions, short
answers, and negative statements
Speaking Asking about nationalities

Getting started

1 Match the countries with the nationality.

American	Argentinian	Australian	Brazilian	British	Canadian	French	German
Indian	Irish	Italian	Japanese	Korean	Mexican	Spanish	Thai

Examples: China–Chinese   Turkey–Turkish

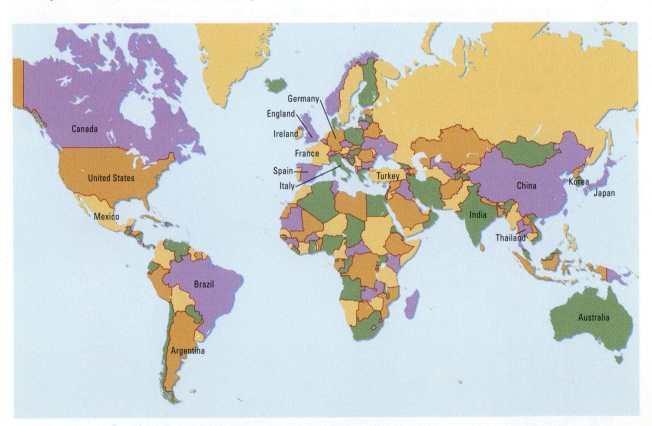

2 🎧 Listen and check your answers. Then listen again and repeat.

3 *PAIRS.* Test your partner.

> France.

> French.
> China.

10

Reading

4 Read the quiz and circle the correct choices.

Are YOU international?

Leisure, Sports, and Entertainment

1. The tango *is / isn't* Argentinian.
2. Jazz *is / isn't* Australian.
3. Judo and kendo *are / aren't* Chinese.

Food and Drink

1. Sashimi and sushi are a) American b) Japanese c) Indian.
2. Paella is a) Italian b) Spanish c) French.
3. Feijoada is a) British b) Turkish c) Brazilian.

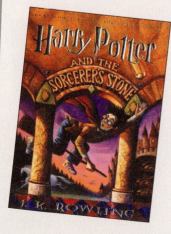
paella

sushi

Famous People

1. Is J. K. Rowling British?
    a) Yes, she is.
    b) No, she isn't.
2. Is top model Gisele Bündchen German?
    a) Yes, she is.
    b) No, she isn't.
3. Are Halle Berry and Ben Affleck Australian?
    a) Yes, they are.
    b) No, they aren't.

5 Listen and check your answers.

3

Grammar focus

1 Study the examples of the verb *be* in negative statements, in *Yes/No* questions, and in short answers.

Jazz **isn't** Australian.	**Is** J. K. Rowling British? Yes, she **is**.
Judo and kendo **aren't** Chinese.	**Are** Halle Berry and Ben Affleck Australian? No, they **aren't**.

2 Look at the examples again. Complete the charts.

Negative statements with *be*

I	**'m not**	
He/She/It	_____	Canadian.
We/You/They	_____	

Yes/No questions with *be*			Short answers
Are	you		Yes, I __am__. / No, I __'m not__.
_____	he/she/it	British?	Yes, she _____. / No, she _____.
_____	we/they/you		Yes, they _____. / No, they _____.

NOTE: 'm not = am not   isn't = is not   aren't = are not

> *Grammar Reference page 142*

3 Rewrite the sentences to make them true.

1. J.K. Rowling is ~~American~~. (British)

   J. K. Rowling isn't American. She's British.

2. Pizza is ~~Turkish~~. (Italian)

   _____

3. Baseball and basketball are ~~Spanish~~. (American)

   _____

4. Enchiladas are ~~French~~. (Mexican)

   _____

5. Origami and ikebana are ~~Russian~~. (Japanese)

   _____

6. Taekwon do is ~~Thai~~. (Korean)

   _____

7. Denzel Washington is ~~British~~. (American)

   _____

8. Cricket and badminton are ~~Australian~~. (British)

   _____

Pronunciation

4 🎧 **Listen. Notice how the voice goes up at the end of these** *Yes/No* **questions.**

Are you Canadian?   Are they Brazilian?

Is he French?   Is she Korean?

Is judo Chinese?   Is pizza Italian?

5 🎧 **Listen again and repeat.**

Writing and Speaking

6 *TWO GROUPS.* **Write an international quiz. Use** *Yes/No* **questions. Group A, look at page 136. Group B, look at page 139.**

7 *PAIRS.* **Find a partner from the other group. Take turns asking each other the questions in your quizzes. Keep score.**

A: *Is the tango Argentinian?*
B: *Yes, it is.*

A: *Is paella Italian?*
B: *No, it isn't. It's Spanish.*

A: *Is J.K. Rowling British?*
B: *Yes, she is.*

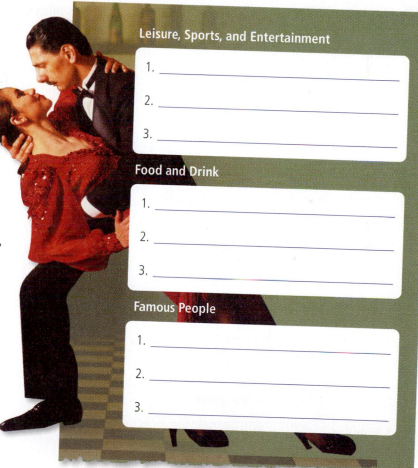

Leisure, Sports, and Entertainment

1. _____

2. _____

3. _____

Food and Drink

1. _____

2. _____

3. _____

Famous People

1. _____

2. _____

3. _____

CONVERSATION TO GO

A: **Are** you **British?**
B: No, I**'m not.** I**'m** half **Irish** and half **American.**

Setting up a home office

Vocabulary Office objects; numbers 20–99
Grammar Plurals; *be* present: *Wh*– questions
Speaking Asking for and giving information

Getting started

1 🎧 **Listen to the numbers and repeat.**

20	30	40	50	60	70	80	90
twenty	thirty	forty	fifty	sixty	seventy	eighty	ninety

2 *PAIRS.* **Write the item numbers from the office supplies catalog next to the correct words.**

a battery #__56__   a briefcase #_____

paper clips #_____   a cell phone #_____

a desk #_____   a dictionary #_____

a fax machine #_____   a file cabinet #_____

a folder #_____   a notepad #_____

a printer #_____   a stapler #_____

3 🎧 **Listen and check your answers. Then listen and repeat.**

Grammar focus

4 **Look at the examples and write the plural form of the nouns in the chart.**

a pen – two pen**s**   a box – two box**es**
    a battery – two batter**ies**

Singular	Plural
a briefcase	briefcases
a desk	
a dictionary	
a stapler	
a fax	

Grammar Reference page 143

POS

#28

#56 DURACELL ALKALINE BATTERY

#92

Order on the Web!
POS.com

Listening

5 🎧 **Listen. Ruth has a home office. She is calling an office supply store. Check (✓) the photos. Which items do Ruth and the salesperson talk about?**

6 🎧 **Listen again. Fill in the prices.**

Item	Price
1 stapler	$7.99
1 box of paper clips	
1 box of folders	
1 pack of notepads	
Subtotal	
Shipping	

POS Professional Office Supplies

#65

#84

#53

#37

#41

#79

#75

#38

#21

Order by phone! 1-800-555-5567

Grammar focus

1 Study the examples of the verb *be* in *Wh-* questions.

> **What is** your name? / **What's** your name?
> **Where is** the fax machine? / **Where's** the fax machine?
> **How much is** the stapler?
> **What are** the shipping charges?
> **Where are** the batteries?
> **How much are** the folders?

2 Look at the examples again. Complete the questions in the chart.

be present: *Wh-* questions		
Singular	_____ your address?	70 Bell Street.
	_____ the cell phone?	In my bag.
	_____ a new desk?	$79.
Plural	_____ your business hours?	9:00 A.M. to 7:00 P.M.
	_____ the folders?	On the desk.
	_____ the supplies?	$63.

Grammar Reference page 143

3 Write questions with *What, Where,* or *How much + be* in the present tense.

1. last name   A: <u>What's your last name</u> ?

     B: It's Palmer.

2. first name   A: _____ ?

     B: It's Irina.

3. email address   A: _____ ?

     B: ipalmer@hotmail.com

4. a box of staples   A: _____ ?

     B: $3.00.

5. the paper clips   A: _____ ?

     B: On the desk.

6. shipping charges   A: _____ ?

     B: $7.00.

Pronunciation

4 🎧 **Listen.** Notice how the voice goes up on the stressed (important) word and down at the end of these *Wh–* questions and answers.

your ad**dress**	What's your ad**dress**?	**Bell** Street	70 **Bell** Street.
your **hours**	What are your **hours**?	**sev**en	Nine to **sev**en.
the **bat**teries	Where are the **bat**teries?	the **desk**	On the **desk**.
the **fax** machine	How much is the **fax** machine?	**dol**lars	Eighty-nine **dol**lars.

5 🎧 **Listen and repeat.**

Speaking and Writing

6 *PAIRS.* **Student A, look at page 136. Student B, stay on this page.**

You're a salesperson at Professional Office Supplies. Student A calls you to place an order. Ask questions. Write the information on the form.

B: *Professional Office Supplies. May I help you?*
A: *Yes, I'd like to order some supplies.*
B: *OK. What's your last name?*

POS Professional Office Supplies

Order Form

Last name, First name _____
Business phone _____
Home phone _____
Email address _____
Office supplies Item/Item # _____
_____
_____

7 Switch roles. **Student B, look at page 136. Student A, stay on this page.**

CONVERSATION TO GO

A: **What's** your name?
B: My name is Bond. James Bond.
A: **What's** your number?
B: 007.

Unit 1 Here's my card.

1 🎧 Listen to the model conversations.

2 *CLASS.* Walk around the room. Greet at least five people.

Unit 2 Meeting people

3 Make a name tag. Write your name and your city. Choose an occupation, but don't write it. (Use your real identity or use your imagination.)

4 🎧 Listen to the model conversation. Then walk around the room. Meet five people and introduce yourself.

5 Introduce one of the people you met to the class.

This is Leticia Barajas. She's from Mexico City. She's a graphic designer.

Name: Claudio Martins

City: São Paulo

Country: Brazil

Name: Leticia Barajas

City: Mexico City

Country: Mexico

Unit 3 Around the world

6 🎧 Listen to the model conversation and look at the photos.

7 **GROUPS OF 3.** Choose one of the photos or think of other international activities, sports, foods, and celebrities. Don't say what you are thinking. Your partners must use *Yes/No* questions to guess.

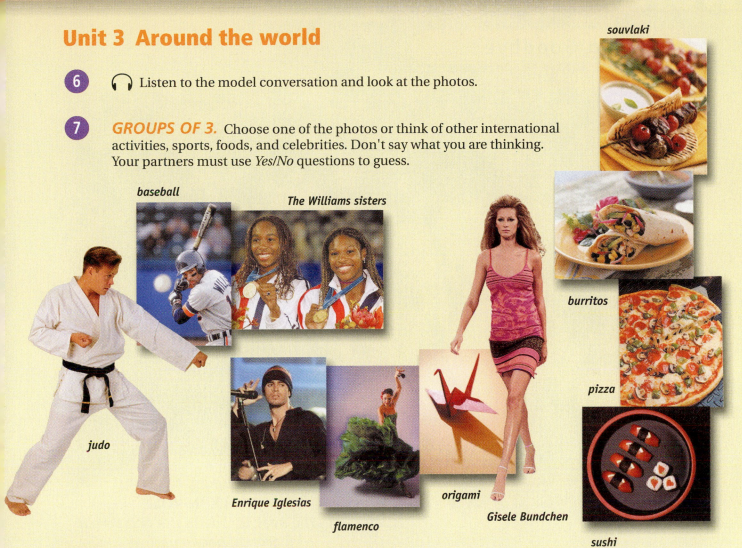

souvlaki

baseball

The Williams sisters

burritos

pizza

judo

Enrique Iglesias

flamenco

origami

Gisele Bundchen

sushi

Unit 4 Setting up a home office

8 🎧 Listen to the model conversation and look at the pictures.

9 **GROUPS OF 4.** Student A, look at page 141. You are the game show host. Students B, C, and D, look at this page and guess the price of each item. The one who has the nearest price without going over "wins" the item. Keep score.

World of Music *1*

Hello Goodbye
John Lennon and Paul McCartney

ROCK 'N ROLL
The Beatles, one of the first British rock groups, began performing in the early 1960s. They eventually produced more #1 hits than any artist before or since.

Vocabulary

1 **PAIRS.** Write the opposite of each word.

1. high   low
2. yes
3. hello
4. small
5. go
6. cheap
7. boring
8. good

20

Listening

2 🎧 **Listen to the song. Which pair of faces matches the story in the song?**

a.   b.   c.

3 🎧 **Listen to the song again. Fill in the blanks.**

Hello Goodbye

You say _____yes_____, I say _____.
You say _____ and I say _____, _____, _____.
Oh, no.
You say _____ and I say _____.

Chorus
Hello, hello.
I don't know why you say goodbye,
I say hello,
Hello, hello.
I don't know why you say goodbye,
I say hello.

I say _____, you say _____.
You say _____, and I say _____ _____ _____.
Oh, no.
You say _____ and I say _____.

Repeat chorus

4 *PAIRS.* **Compare your answers.**

Speaking

5 *GROUPS OF 3.* **Discuss these questions.**

The singer is "talking" to someone. Who is it?

What are they talking about? Why can't they agree?

21

Favorite things

Vocabulary Free-time activities
Grammar Possessive adjectives and possessive 's
Speaking Talking about people and favorite things

A

B

D

Getting started

1 Look at the photos. Check (✓) the five things in the box that you see.

a baseball game ____   a book ____   a department store ____   a magazine ____   a market ✓

a movie ____   a museum ____   a newspaper ____   a restaurant ____   a TV show ____

2 *PAIRS.* Write the words from Exercise 1 under the correct verbs. You will use some words more than one time.

read	go to	watch
a book	a museum	a TV show

3 🎧 Listen and check your answers.

C

E

Listening

4 🎧 **Listen to the interviews. What does each speaker like? Write the letter of the photo.**

Margarita E

David ◯

Min ◯

José ◯

5 *PAIRS.* Compare your answers.

6 🎧 Listen again. Are the sentences true or false? Write *T* or *F* next to each one.

1. Bob Samples is a radio announcer. T
2. Tim and Margarita's favorite restaurant is a Greek restaurant.
3. Their children's favorite food is hamburgers.
4. David and his wife's favorite thing is to go to the beach.
5. José's favorite things to read are travel magazines.
6. Min's favorite store is Macy's.

Grammar focus

1 Study the examples of possessive adjectives and possessive 's.

My favorite thing to do is travel.	**Our** favorite restaurant is *Chez Paul*.
What's **your** favorite magazine?	
Her favorite food is French.	**Their** favorite magazine is *People*.
Its food is excellent.	
Alberto's favorite thing is sports.	**The Yangs'** favorite store is **Macy's**.

2 Look at the examples again. Complete the chart.

Possessive adjectives				Possessive 's
I	_my_	we	_____	David _David's_
you	_____			the Garcias _____
he	_____			Maria _____
she	_____	they	_____	
it	_____			**NOTE:** Do not say X *the favorite thing of Alberto*

> **Grammar Reference page 143**

3 Complete the sentences with a possessive adjective or 's.

_____My_____ name is Rachel. This is _____ friend. _____
  1. (I)   **2. (I)**   **3. (She)**

name is Ana. _____ favorite store is Zara.
                4. (We)

John and Sue are _____ friends. _____ favorite restaurant is the *Hard*
                        5. (we)   **6. (They)**

Rock Café. _____ favorite movie is *The Lord of the Rings*. _____ special
                7. (John)   **8. (It)**

effects are excellent. _____ favorite books are *Cry to Heaven* and *Dracula*.
                            9. (Sue)

Who are _____ friends? What are _____ favorite things to do?
            10. (you)   **11. (they)**

Pronunciation

4 🎧 Listen. Notice the weak pronunciation of the possessive adjectives.

my friend	This is my friend.	his name	His name is John.
his wife	This is his wife.	her name	Her name is Sue.
your favorite	What's your favorite city?	my favorite	My favorite city is New York.
our favorite	Our favorite restaurant is Italian.	their pizza	Their pizza is great!

5 🎧 Listen and repeat.

Speaking

6 **BEFORE YOU SPEAK.** Write three more things in the first column. Then fill in the information about your favorite things in the second column.

Your favorite . . . ?

	My favorite . . .	_____'s favorite . . .	_____'s favorite . . .
movie			
food			
TV show			

7 **GROUPS OF 3.** Take turns asking one another about favorite things. Take notes in the chart.

A: *What's your favorite movie?*
B: *My favorite movie is* Star Wars—*all of them!*
C: *My favorite movies are* Amélie *and* The Ring.

8 Tell the class about one of your partners' favorite things.

Writing

9 Choose someone you know, such as a classmate or a friend. Write a paragraph about his or her favorite things. Use possessive adjectives and 's, and some of the vocabulary from this unit.

CONVERSATION TO GO

A: What's **your** favorite music?
B: Mozart.

Lesson A

Interesting places

Vocabulary Adjectives to describe places in a city
Grammar *There is/There are*
Speaking Talking about places you know

Getting started

1 ***PAIRS.*** **Use the words in the box to complete the sentences.**

cheap	crowded	delicious	friendly	~~interesting~~

1. Tourists go to Chinatown in New York because it's ____interesting____.

2. Some things are _____.
   For example, you can buy a shirt for $10.

3. The people are _____.
   They always talk to you.

4. I love the street food. It's _____.

5. It's _____ on Saturday.
   There are lots of people.

2 ***PAIRS.*** **Match each adjective with its opposite.**

1. cheap _d_   a. unfriendly
2. crowded ____   b. bad
3. big ____   c. empty
4. friendly ____ d. expensive
5. interesting ____ e. terrible
6. good ____   f. boring
7. wonderful ____ g. small

3 ***PAIRS.*** **Use the words in Exercise 2 to describe a place you know.**

Soho, in New York City, is interesting. There are expensive shops and good restaurants . . .

Back Forward Stop Refresh Home AutoFill Print Mail

Address: @ http://www.html

Favorites History Search Scrapbook Page Holder

Real places by real people

Portobello Road

by Simon Bean, London

I love Portobello Road. It's one of London's main tourist attractions. There aren't any big department stores, but there is an interesting market on Fridays and Saturdays. You can buy everything from fruit and vegetables to cheap clothes, CDs, books, and antiques.

Can you get good coffee there? Yes! There are lots of cafés. My favorite is the Portuguese Café. They have great coffee and delicious cakes.

What about food? There are some wonderful restaurants, and they're usually crowded on the weekend. I love the Market Tavern. They have excellent music on Fridays and Saturdays, and there are lots of friendly people.

Reading

4 **PAIRS.** Describe the photos of Portobello Road. Use the adjectives in Exercise 2.

5 Read about Portobello Road. Are the sentences true or false? Write **T** or **F** next to each one.

1. There is a big museum. F
2. There is a market two days a week.
3. There aren't any cafés on Portobello Road.
4. There isn't music in the Market Tavern on the weekend.

Don't listen to the travel agents.
Listen to the people who live there.

Listening

6 🎧 Listen to Maria tell Paul about Harvard Square. Check (✓) the things they talk about.

people _____

a subway station _____

the university _____

beautiful buildings _____

office buildings _____

old churches _____

new stores _____

interesting restaurants _____

delicious drinks _____

the Tea Room _____

a fruit market _____

a street musician _____

coffee bars _____

6

Grammar focus

1 Study the examples with *there is* and *there are*.

> **There is/There's** an interesting market on the weekend.
> **There are** some wonderful restaurants.
>
> **There isn't** a movie theater.
> **There aren't** any big museums.
>
> **Is there** a good café? Yes, **there is**. / No, **there isn't**.
> **Are there** any interesting restaurants? Yes, **there are**. / No, **there aren't**.

2 Look at the examples again. Complete the rules in the chart.

There is/There are	
Affirmative statements	**Negative statements**
Use *there* + _____ + singular nouns.	Use *there* + _____ + singular nouns.
Use *there* + _____ + plural nouns.	Use *there* + _____ + plural nouns.
Yes/No questions	**Short answers**
Use _____ + *there . . .?* with singular nouns.	Use *Yes, there* _____ and *No, there* _____ with singular nouns.
Use _____ + *there . . .?* with plural nouns.	Use *Yes, there* _____ and *No, there* _____ with plural nouns.
NOTE: We usually use *any* with *Are there . . .?* and *There aren't . . . .*	

> **Grammar Reference page 143**

3 Describe this picture. Write five sentences. Use *there is/isn't* and *there are/aren't*.

cars	good cafés	interesting stores
a market	~~people~~	a small hotel

There are some people on the street.

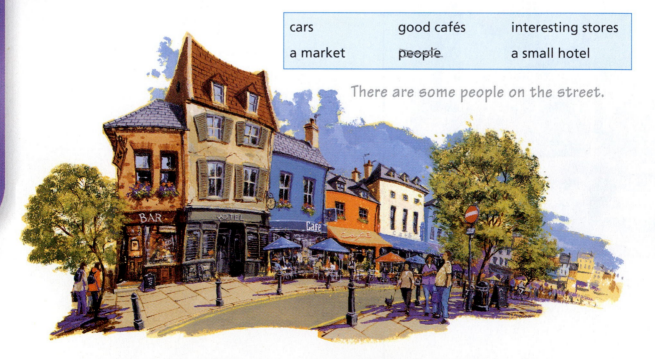

Pronunciation

4 🎧 **Listen. Notice the pronunciation of the voiced *th* sound, /ð/.**

there	**th**ere's	**the** weekend

There are good cafés.   **Th**ere's a market on **the** weekend.

Are **th**ere any restaurants?   Yes, **th**ere are.

Is **th**ere a museum?   No, **th**ere isn't.

5 🎧 **Listen again and repeat.**

Speaking

6 *BEFORE YOU SPEAK.* **You are going to talk to your partner about his or her favorite part of a city. Write three more questions below.**

7 *PAIRS.* **Take turns. Find out the name of the city and your partner's favorite part of the city. Then ask your questions. Take notes.**

City: _____ Favorite part of the city: _____

Are there any interesting cafés? _____

Is there a good music club? _____

What do you like most about (the). . . ? _____

_____

_____

_____

8 **Tell the class about your partner's favorite place in Exercise 7.**

Marta likes the French Quarter in New Orleans because there are . . .

Writing

9 **Look at the "Real Places" website on pages 26 and 27. Write a review of your favorite place in a city or town. Use *there is/isn't* and *there are/aren't* to describe the special details.**

CONVERSATION TO GO

A: **Are there** any good cafés here?

B: Yes, **there are**.

29

Office...or living room?

Vocabulary Furniture in an office or living room
Grammar Prepositions of location
Speaking Telling someone where things are in a room

Getting started

1 **PAIRS.** Write the numbers of the items in the picture next to the correct words.

an armchair ____	a bookcase ____	a cabinet ____	a calendar _1_
a chair ____	a computer ____	a desk ____	a lamp ____
a plant ____	a printer ____	a sofa ____	a stereo ____
a table ____	a telephone ____	a wastebasket ____	a window ____

2 🎧 Listen and check your answers.

30

Pronunciation

3 🎧 Listen to the words. Notice the number of syllables and the stress. Write each word in the correct group.

○	○ ○	○ ○ ○	○ ○ ○
chair lamp	armchair		

4 🎧 Listen and check your answers. Then listen again and repeat.

5 *PAIRS.* Take turns pointing to an item in the picture on page 30.

> What's this?

> It's a table.

Listening

6 🎧 Listen to Christine talk to two moving men. Look at the picture on page 30. Check (✓) the items that you hear.

7 🎧 Listen again. Underline the words to make the sentences true.

1. Christine **is / isn't** sure about where she wants the furniture.
2. Christine wants to use the room as a **living room / home office**.

Grammar focus

1 **Study the examples of prepositions of location.**

Put the desk **in front of** the window.
I'd like the computer **on** the desk, please.
Put the plant **next to** the sofa.
Put the armchair **opposite** the desk.

The calendar is **above** the sofa.
There's a stereo **in** the cabinet.
The wastebasket is **under** the desk.

2 **Look at the examples again. Where is the ball? Write the correct preposition for each picture.**

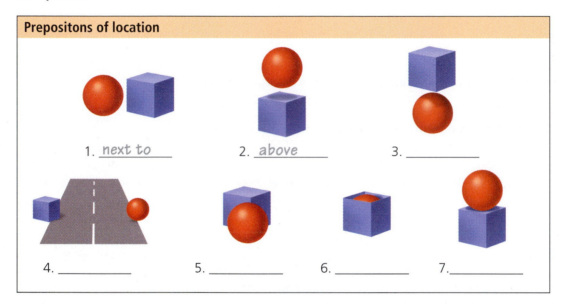

Prepositons of location

1. _next to_   2. _above_   3. _____

4. _____   5. _____   6. _____   7._____

> **Grammar Reference page 144**

3 **PAIRS.** Say a sentence. Look at the picture. Say the sentence again with the correct preposition.

A: There's a table opposite the door.
B: No. There's a table next to the door.

1. There's a table ~~opposite~~ the door. *(next to)*
2. The telephone is in front of the desk.
3. There's a wastebasket next to the desk
4. I put the stereo on the cabinet.
5. There's a plant in front of the sofa.
6. The printer is next to the desk.
7. There's a cabinet above the bookcase.
8. I put my favorite armchair next to the desk.
9. There's a calendar opposite the sofa.

Speaking

4 ***BEFORE YOU SPEAK.*** Think about your office or living room. Draw windows, the door, and one piece of furniture in the room. Then exchange books with a partner.

My floor plan for _____.

5 ***PAIRS.*** Take turns describing your office or living room. Describe the things in your room. Use prepositions to talk about their locations. Your partner will draw the furniture and objects on the floor plan in your book.

There's a table in front of the sofa. Opposite the sofa, there's . . .

6 Show the floor plan to your partner when you're finished. Is everything in the right place?

Writing

7 Draw a floor plan of an office or living room you know and write a description of it. Use the prepositions of location from this unit.

CONVERSATION TO GO

A: Where is the phone?
B: It's **on** the desk—I think.

Celebrations

Vocabulary Holiday celebrations
Grammar Simple present: affirmative statements
Speaking Talking about holidays

Thanksgiving Day

New Year's Day

Getting started

1 Match each verb on the left with the correct group of words. Use each letter only one time.

1. cook __e__
2. dance ___
3. drink ___
4. eat ___
5. get up ___
6. give ___
7. go ___
8. play ___
9. visit ___
10. wash ___

a. to salsa music, with someone
b. a friend, your family, a place
c. the dishes, your hands
d. for a walk, to bed
e. lunch, dinner, food
f. ice cream, pizza, a meal
g. juice, soda, water
h. a present, money
i. a game, cards, the piano
j. at 8:00, in the morning

2 Look at the photos of some important celebrations. Guess. In what countries are these celebrations? When do they take place? See page 141 for answers.

3 *PAIRS.* Describe the celebrations in the photos. Use words from Exercise 1.

On Thanksgiving, they eat a special meal.
On New Year's Day, . . .
During Carnaval, . . .

Carnaval

Reading

4 *PAIRS.* Read Amy's letter to her Japanese pen pal, Fumino, about Thanksgiving.

November 21

Dear Fumino,

Next week is Thanksgiving. It's an important national holiday in the U.S. We celebrate it on the fourth Thursday in November. Everyone in my family eats all day—I love it!

My mother cooks the food. She gets up at six o'clock in the morning to begin! My brother and I get up at about nine o'clock and help my mother in the kitchen. A lot of our relatives come to our house, too. We eat a big meal at two o'clock. After the meal, we always have coffee and dessert. Then we wash the dishes!

Later in the afternoon my father and brother watch football on TV. The kids play card games. My mother and I go for a walk. I'll send a photo.

Write soon!

Amy

5 Read Amy's letter again. Correct the mistakes in the sentences.
1. My mother gets up at ~~seven~~ six o'clock.
2. My father cooks the meal.
3. My brother and I get up at eight o'clock.
4. We eat at five o'clock.
5. My mother and brother watch football on TV.
6. The kids play the piano.
7. My father and I go for a walk.

6 Is there a holiday in your country like Thanksgiving Day?

8

Grammar focus

1 **Study the examples of the simple present tense affirmative statements.**

I **wash** the dishes.	She **goes** for a walk.
My mother **gets up** at 6:00.	We **eat** at 2:00.
My father **watches** football.	She **cooks** the turkey.

2 **Look at the examples again. Complete the rules in the chart.**

Simple present: affirmative statements

For third person singular subjects, such as *he, she*, or *it*, add _____ to the verb.

But add _____ to *do, go*, and verbs that end in *–ch, -s, -sh, -x* for third person singular subjects.

NOTE: Look at the way the verb *have* changes:
I *have* breakfast at 10:00.
He *has* breakfast at 10:00.

Grammar Reference page 144

3 **Read the sentences about how Fumino celebrates New Year's Day in Japan. Underline the correct verb forms.**

1. We **get up / gets** up at 6:00.
2. My father **go / goes** for a walk.
3. I **visit / visits** my friends in the morning.
4. My mother **cook / cooks** lunch.
5. My father **drink / drinks** sake.
6. We **eat / eats** a special dish called osechi.
7. My brother usually **watch / watches** TV.
8. Our parents **give / gives** us money.
9. I **play / plays** cards with my parents.

Pronunciation

4 🎧 Listen. Notice the three different pronunciations of the third-person singular *-s/-es* ending.

visits /s/	plays /z/	watches /ɪz/
gets		

5 🎧 Listen to more verbs. Write them in the correct sound group.

6 🎧 Listen and check your answers. Then listen again and repeat.

Speaking

7 *BEFORE YOU SPEAK.* Think of a holiday that your family celebrates each year. Write the things that you and your family do.

> **Holiday :** Mother's Day
> Peggy and I get up early
> make breakfast, cook dinner
> Dad buys flowers

8 *PAIRS.* Take turns. Describe the things that you and your family do. Don't tell your partner the name of your holiday! Your partner will guess which celebration it is.

My sister and I get up early and make breakfast for my mother. We also cook dinner in the evening. My Dad buys my mother flowers.

Writing

9 Write a letter to a friend about a special day or a holiday you celebrate every year. Use the simple present and some of the vocabulary from this unit.

CONVERSATION TO GO

A: My dad **plays** cards and **watches** TV.
B: Oh? My dad **cooks** and **washes** the dishes!

Unit 5 Favorite things

1 🎧 Listen to the model conversation.

2 **GROUPS OF 4.** Student A, say your favorite thing to do, or your favorite kind of restaurant, or your favorite food. Student B, report Student A's information. Then say your favorite thing to do, your favorite kind of restaurant, or your favorite food. Then Students C and D continue.

Unit 6 Interesting places

3 🎧 Listen to the model conversation and look at the charts.

4 **GROUPS OF 3.** Take turns. Think of a city, a town, or a neighborhood (an area in a town or city). Say three things about it. Your partners will guess the place.

It's	very	busy	There is	a	beautiful	beach
	really	big friendly	There are	some	busy	market
	super	interesting		many	famous	museum
	a little	cheap		a lot of	interesting	cafés
		expensive			nice	parks
		small				restaurants
		boring				stores
		unfriendly				cars
		quiet				people
		crowded				things to do

Unit 7 Office . . . or living room?

5 🎧 Listen to the model conversation and look at the picture.

6 *GROUPS OF 3.* Take turns. Choose one item in the picture. Say a sentence about its location. Your partners will name the item. Keep score. Who's the "fastest listener"?

Unit 8 Celebrations

7 *GROUPS OF 3.* You will have two minutes. Write the names of six holidays and special celebrations. Write each one on a small piece of paper. Fold the papers in half and mix them all together. Exchange papers with another group.

8 🎧 Listen to the model conversation.

9 *GROUPS OF 3.* Take turns. Pick a folded paper. You will have 30 seconds. Give information about the holiday, but don't say the name. If no one can guess, return the paper to the pile. Correct answers receive 1 point. Keep score.

Lesson A

The collectors

Vocabulary Objects people collect; numbers 100–1,000,000
Grammar Simple present: *Yes/No* questions, short answers, and negative statements
Speaking Talking about possessions

The Biggest Garfield Collection

Do you collect things? Mike Drysdale and Gayle Brennan do. They're from California, and they collect Garfield souvenirs. It's their passion!

Mike and Gayle don't just collect a few Garfield things. They share their house with 3,000 Garfield souvenirs! In fact, their house is like a Garfield museum. They don't have souvenirs in only one room—they have Garfield posters, toys, comics, and clothes in every room! They started their collection in 1994 when Gayle bought a Garfield bed for their cats.

Jim Davis created Garfield in 1978, and now 220 million people read the comic strip. However, Jim Davis doesn't have a cat because his wife doesn't like them.

Getting started

1 *PAIRS.* **What kinds of things do people collect? Make a list.**

2 **Check (✓) the words that you see in the photo.**

a book ____	a clock ✓	a doll ____	a photo album ____
a picture ____	a plate ____	a postcard ____	a poster ____
a stuffed animal ____	a toy ____	a T-shirt ____	a video ____

3 🎧 **Listen and repeat.**

4 **PAIRS.** Write the words for each number.

100 = _one hundred_   1,000 = _____

10,000 = _____   100,000 = _____

1,000,000 = _one million_

5 🎧 Listen and repeat.

Reading

6 Read the article about the collectors. Then complete the sentences with the correct information.

| comic strip | Garfield | million | museum | souvenirs |

1. _____Garfield_____ is a comic strip character.
2. Mike and Gayle collect Garfield _____.
3. Their house is like a Garfield _____.
4. Jim Davis writes the Garfield _____.
5. About 220 _____ people read the comic.

Pronunciation

7 🎧 Listen to these words. Notice the stressed (strong) syllable in each word.

album   col**lect**   **hun**dred

million   mu**se**um   **an**imal

thousand   **pic**ture   **pos**ter

8 🎧 Listen again. This time, notice the sound of the vowel in the weak syllables.

9 🎧 Now listen and repeat.

9

Grammar focus

1 Study the examples of the simple present tense negative statements, *Yes/No* questions, and short answers.

> I **don't collect** posters.
> His wife **doesn't like** cats.
> We **don't read** the comics.
>
> **Does** Jim Davis **like** cats?   Yes, he **does**.
> **Do** you **collect** Garfield souvenirs? No, I **don't**.

2 Look at the examples again. Complete the sentences in the charts with the correct form of the verb *have*.

Negative statements			
I/You/We/They	don't (do not)	_____	a photo album.
He/She/It	doesn't (does not)	_____	baseball cards.

Yes/No questions				Short answers
_____	you	_____	Garfield souvenirs?	Yes, I do. No, I don't.
_____	Jim Davis	_____	a cat?	Yes, he does. No, he doesn't.

> **Grammar Reference page 144**

3 Complete the questions and the answers.

1. A: _Do you collect_ (collect) toys?

   B: No, I _don't_. I _collect_ T-shirts from concerts.

2. A: _____ (have) a photo collection?

   B: Yes, they _____. But they _____ (not have) any photo albums.

3. A: _____ (like) baseball cards?

   B: No, he _____. He _____ (not like) sports.

4. A: _____ (collect) postcards?

   B: Yes, I _____. But I _____ (not collect) postcards from my own country!

5. A: _____ (read) Garfield comics?

   B: Yes, I _____. But my husband _____ (not read) them.

6. A: _____ (have) any *Star Wars* T-shirts?

   B: No, he _____. But he _____ (have) 2,000 *Star Wars* toys.

Speaking

4 **BEFORE YOU SPEAK.** Fill out the questionnaire. What do you collect? How many do you have? You can use *about* (for example, *about 100*) or *over* (for example, *over 50*).

5 **PAIRS.** Ask each other about the special things you collect. Do you collect any of the same things?

A: *Do you collect books?*
B: *Yes, I do. / No, I don't.*

A: *Do you have a lot of books?*
B: *Yes, I do. I have over 300. /*
     No, I don't. I have about 15.

Are you a collector?

Do you collect . . . ?	How many do you have?
books ☐	
CDs ☐	
photos ☐	
videos ☐	
clocks ☐	
plates ☐	
toys ☐	
posters ☐	
postcards ☐	
other _____	

Writing

6 Write a paragraph about one of the following:

• a collection you have
• a collection that someone you know has
• a collection in a museum or gallery

Describe the objects and talk about how many there are. Use the simple present and some of the vocabulary from this unit.

CONVERSATION TO GO

A: **Do** you **have** a lot of stuffed animals?
B: **Yes**, I **do**. I **have** over 400!

UNIT 10

The modern world

Vocabulary Words related to communication
Grammar Simple present: *Wh–* questions
Speaking Talking about ways of communicating

A

B

C

Getting started

1 **Look at pictures A–C. Match them with the sentences.**

1. They have meetings in person. ____
2. He uses the Internet to do his homework. ____
3. She's on the phone. ____

2 *PAIRS.* **How do your friends communicate with you: In person? By email? On the phone?**

3 **Use the verbs in the box to complete the sentences in the questionnaire.**

book	buy	contact	do
get	listen	research	~~use~~

The Modern World magazine

Are you an Internet Person?

1 Do you ___use___ the Internet?
a) yes
b) no

2 Do you _____ books
a) by mail?
b) on the Internet?
c) in person?

3 Do you _____ your banking
a) on the phone?
b) on the Internet?
c) in person?

4 Do you _____ hotels or flights
a) on the phone?
b) on the Internet?
c) through a travel agent?

5 Do you _____ friends
a) on the phone?
b) by email?
c) in person?

6 Do you _____ to music
a) at home?
b) on the Internet?
c) at concerts?

7 Do you _____ your news
a) from TV?
b) on the Internet?
c) from the newspaper?

8 Do you _____ information
a) at the library?
b) on the Internet?
c) by speaking to people?

Listening

4 🎧 Listen to Giselle and Thomas discuss a magazine quiz on modern communication. Check (✓) the methods of communication they talk about.

the phone ____   the Internet ____   TV ____
magazines ____   newspapers ____   radio ____

5 🎧 Listen again and complete the statements with the numbers in the box. You will not use all of the numbers.

| 33 | 43 | 66 | 80 | 98 | 100 |

Of Americans who have the Internet, . . .

1. _____% use email to contact friends.

2. _____% also use the phone to contact friends.

3. _____% use the Internet to research hotels.

4. _____% use the Internet to make hotel reservations.

Grammar focus

1 **Study the examples of the simple present tense *Wh-* questions.**

> **How do** we **communicate**?
> **When does** she **use** the Internet?
> **What do** these results **tell** us?
>
> **Why does** he **book** flights online?
> **Where do** they **get** their news?

2 **Look at the examples again. Underline the correct word to complete each rule.**

> **Simple present: *Wh-* questions**
>
> For *Wh-* questions in the simple present with *he*, *she*, and *it*, use **do / does**.
>
> For *Wh-* questions in the simple present with *I*, *you*, *we*, and *they*, use **do / does**.
>
> After *do* or *does*, use **the infinitive / base form** of the verb.

> *Grammar Reference page 144*

3 **Read the answers and write the questions.**

1. A: ___How do you buy DVDs___?
   B: I buy DVDs online.
2. A: _____?
   B: He uses the Internet in the evening.
3. A: _____?
   B: She listens to music at home.
4. A: _____?
   B: They get the news from TV.
5. A: _____?
   B: We use the Internet to do research.

Pronunciation

4 **Listen. Notice the weak pronunciation of *do* and *does* and the pronouns and the way some words are linked together.**

Do you watch	Do you watch TV?
How do you	How do you contact friends?
When do you	When do you use the Internet?
Does he use	Does he use email?
Where does he	Where does he buy books?
When does she	When does she listen to music?

5 **Listen and repeat.**

Speaking

6 **BEFORE YOU SPEAK.** Create your own interview to find out how your classmates use the Internet. Use *How* or *Where* to complete the questions.

Do you use the Internet?	Name _____
_____ do you buy books?	_____
_____ do you do your banking?	_____
_____ do you book hotels or flights?	_____
_____ do you contact friends?	_____
_____ do you listen to music?	_____
_____ do you get your news?	_____
_____ do you do research?	_____

7 **PAIRS.** Take turns. Interview each other. Write your notes on your interview form. Then describe your partner to the class. Use the information below.

Ana Maria uses the Internet to do almost everything! She buys books on the Internet, and she uses email to contact her friends. She likes to do things very quickly.

If your partner answered mostly . . .
on the phone, on TV, in newspapers and magazines:
He or she likes to do things more traditionally.
on the Internet:
He or she likes to do things very quickly.
in person:
He or she likes to do things more personally.

Writing

8 Think about different ways of communicating. Write a paragraph describing a typical week for you and the different ways you communicate with others (friends, family, business colleagues).

CONVERSATION TO GO

A: **When do** you **use** the Internet?
B: All the time!

Traveling

Vocabulary Things you take on vacation; types of transportation
Grammar *A, an, some, any*
Speaking Talking about vacations

Lesson A

Getting started

1. *PAIRS.* Write the letter of each object next to the correct word on the list.

2. 🎧 Listen and check your answers. Then listen and repeat.

3. *PAIRS.* Which objects on the list do you always take on vacation?

I always take a guidebook and a credit card.

Things to take on vacation

hiking boots ___I___
an umbrella _____
a map _____
sweaters _____
a bathing suit _____
a beach towel _____
sunglasses _____
a phrasebook _____
a guidebook _____
books to read _____
a camera _____
film _____
an alarm clock _____
a portable CD player _____
CDs _____
a credit card _____
travelers checks _____

4 **Check (✓) the types of transportation you see.**

- ❑ bicycle
- ❑ boat
- ❑ bus
- ❑ car
- ❑ motorcycle
- ❑ plane
- ❑ subway
- ❑ taxi
- ❑ train
- ❑ trolley

5 *PAIRS.* **Take turns asking and answering these questions:**

How do you usually travel on vacation? By car? By train? By plane?
How do you usually get around town? On foot? By bus? By car?

Reading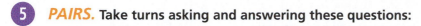

6 *PAIRS.* **Look at the photo of Tim Lee, a writer for travel guidebooks. Predict:**

What six things from the list on page 48 does Tim always take with him on vacation?
What two things does he *not* take?

7 **Read the article and check your answers.**

On Vacation with Tim Lee

I always pack a camera, some film, and a credit card. An alarm
   clock is important because I get up early to visit places
   before the crowds arrive . . . and to take good pictures. I also
   take some sweaters—in case it gets cold or windy! And I
   pack some books to read.
I never pack a portable CD player because I like listening to the people when I'm in a
   different country. I may be a guidebook writer, but I don't take any guidebooks.
   They're heavy!
I always fly to where I'm going on vacation. But when I'm there, I take a train,
   because I have more time, and I like to see the countryside. I never take a bus
   because it's too slow and it isn't comfortable.

8 *PAIRS.* **Read the article again. Answer the questions.**

What does Tim pack to make sure he gets up early?
What does Tim pack in case it gets cold or windy?
Why does Tim take the train on vacation?
Why doesn't Tim take a bus?

Grammar focus

Alaska

1 **Study the examples with *a*, *an*, *some*, and *any*.**

> I always pack **a** notepad.
> **An** alarm clock is important.
> I pack **some** books.
> I don't pack **a** portable CD player.
> I don't take **any** guidebooks.
> Do you take **any** traveler's checks?

2 **Look at the examples again. Complete the rules in the chart.**

a, an, some, any
Use _____ or _____ to talk about one thing (singular).
Use _____ to talk about more than one thing (plural), but when the number is not important.
Use _____ with plural negatives and questions.
NOTE: Use *an* before a vowel sound: *an* alarm clock.

> **Grammar Reference page 145**

3 **Complete the sentences with *a*, *an*, *some* or *any*.**

1. Roberta usually takes ___*some*___ CDs.

2. Do you always pack _____ umbrella?

3. I don't pack _____ books.

4. Ana wants to buy _____ guidebooks.

5. I always pack _____ alarm clock.

6. Paulo never takes _____ phrasebook.

7. I always take _____ beach towel.

8. We don't have _____ travelers checks.

Pronunciation

4 🎧 **Listen. Notice the weak pronunciation of *a*, *an*, *some*, and *any*.**

I always pack a camera.
An alarm clock is important.
I pack some books.
I don't pack any guidebooks.

I never take a CD player.
I don't take an umbrella.
I take some sweaters.
Do you take any travelers checks?

5 🎧 **Listen again and repeat.**

Speaking

Rome

Kenya

6 *GROUPS OF 3.* **Choose one of the photos. Decide how to travel to this place, what to pack, and how to travel once you are there. Take notes about your decisions.**

7 **Tell the class about your travel plans.**

We're going to Alaska. We're flying there. We're packing some sweaters. We're going to travel by car when we are there.

Writing

8 **Tim Lee is going to a new place to write his next guidebook, and you're going with him! Choose the destination and make the plans.**

Write a paragraph about:

• the things that you want to pack.
• how you want to travel from your home to your destination.
• how you want to travel when you are there.

Use *a, an, some, any,* and some of the vocabulary from this unit. Use these sentence starters: *I want to . . . / I'm going to . . .*

CONVERSATION TO GO

A: I usually travel **by car** and take **some CDs**!
B: What?

51

Shopping

Vocabulary Clothes and sizes
Grammar Demonstrative adjectives: *this, that, these, those*
Speaking Asking for information in a store

Lesson A

Getting started

1 Look at the pictures. Match the pictures to the correct words in the box.

boots ____	coat _A_	jacket ____	pants ____	shirt ____	shoes ___
shorts ____	skirt ____	sneakers ____	suit ____	sweater ____	T-shirt ____

2 *PAIRS.* Talk about these questions.
Do you like shopping for clothes?
Where do you buy your clothes?
What kind of clothes do you usually shop for?

3 Complete the table with the words in the box.

extra large   extra small   large   medium   small

Clothing sizes in the U.S.					
Women's sizes	____	____	____	____	____
	4	6–8	10–12	14–16	18–20
Men's sizes					
jackets		34–36	38–40	42–44	46–48
pants		28–30	32–34	36–38	40–42

Listening

4 Listen to the conversation between the salesperson and the customer. Check (✓) the words in Exercise 1 that you hear.

5 Listen to the conversation again. Underline the correct answers.

The customer wants:
1. a sweater in **small / medium / large**.
2. black pants in a size **8 / 12 / 14**.
3. **a blue / a green / a red** skirt.
4. a black **jacket / raincoat / boots**.

Pronunciation

6 Listen. Notice the focus word—the most important word—in each sentence. The voice jumps up or down to make this word stand out.

Can I **help** you?

Do you have this shirt in **large**?

The **blue** shirt?

No, the **green** one.

We only have it in **medium**.

7 Listen again and repeat.

53

12

Grammar focus

1 Study the examples with the demonstrative adjectives *this*, *that*, *these*, and *those*.

> **This** skirt is nice.
> **That** skirt in the window is very popular.
>
> Do you have **these** pants in black?
> **Those** pants near the door are on sale.

2 Look at the examples again. Use *near* or *not near* to complete each rule in the chart.

> **Demonstrative adjectives: *this, that, these, those***
>
> *This* refers to a person or thing _____ you.
> *That* refers to a person or thing _____ you.
>
> *These* refers to people or things _____ you.
> *Those* refers to people or things _____ you.

> *Grammar Reference page 145*

3 **PAIRS.** Look at the picture and complete the conversation with *this*, *that*, *these*, and *those*.

A: Hello. Can I help you?
B: Yes. Do you have ___this___ shirt in blue?
A: No, I'm sorry. But _____ shirt over there comes in blue.
B: No, thanks. I also need a black sweater. Do you have any in large?
A: Yes, right here. _____ sweaters are really nice.
B: OK. I'll try one on. Also, do you sell sneakers?
A: Yes. And the sneakers near the cashier are on sale!
B: Great. _____ sneakers are cool. Thanks for your help.

4 🎧 Listen and check your answers.

Speaking

5   *PAIRS.* **Role-play a conversation between a salesperson and a customer. Student A, you are the salesperson. Look at page 137. Student B, you are the customer.**

Buy three items on this page.

- Ask for an item.
- Ask for the color you want and the size you need.
- Ask about the price.

6   **Now, switch roles.**

7   **Tell the class what you bought.**

I bought a blue sweater in a medium.

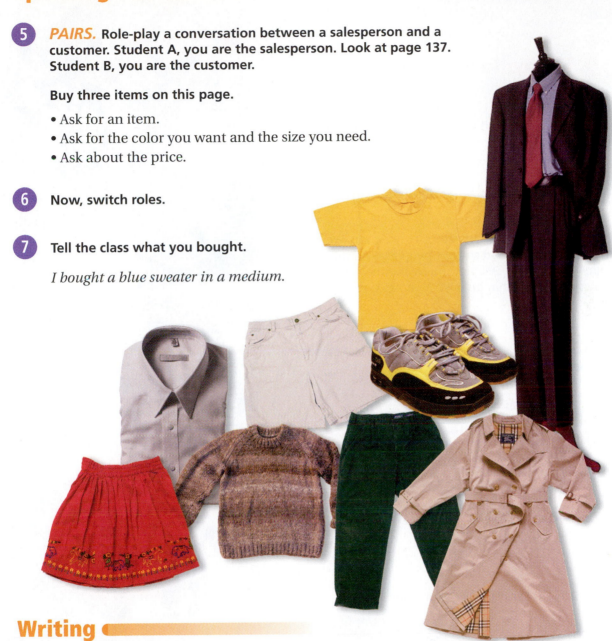

Writing

8   **Imagine you need some new clothes (for example, for a new job, for a party, or for a trip). Write a list of things you want to get. Include the items, colors, and sizes you need.**

CONVERSATION TO GO

A: **Can I help you?**
B: Do you have **this** sweater in **large**, **medium**, and **small**?

Unit 9 The collectors

1 You are a collector. Decide which one of the items in the photos you collect. Write your information on a piece of paper.

2 🎧 Listen to the model conversation.

3 *CLASS.* You are at a collectors' convention. Walk around the room and ask five people about the items they collect. Ask how many they have and why they collect that item. Write notes on the piece of paper.

4 Who collects the same items? Do they collect them for the same reasons?

Unit 10 The modern world

5 🎧 Listen to the model conversation.

6 *GROUPS OF 3.* Take turns. Student A, you are a visitor from another planet. Choose one of the communication tools in the box. Ask four questions to find out about the tool. Use *Why, When, Where, How,* and *do/does* to form your questions.

Communication Tools		
cell phone	computer	newspapers
pager	radio	telephone
television		

Unit 11 Traveling

7 🎧 Listen to the model conversation.

8 Think of a place to go on vacation. Imagine that you go there every year. Write down three things you always take with you and one thing that you never take.

9 *GROUPS OF 4.* Take turns. Tell your group the vacation place. The group must guess the things you always take and the thing you never take.

Unit 12 Shopping

10 🎧 Listen to the model conversation and look at the pictures.

11 *PAIRS.* Role-play. Student A, you are the salesperson. Help the customer decide which items to buy. Student B, you are the customer. You need to buy new clothes. Look at the pictures and ask the salesperson for help. Then switch roles.

World of Music 2

Up on the Roof
The Drifters

Vocabulary

1 Use the words and phrases in the box to complete the conversations.

fresh and sweet	getting me down
~~hustling crowds~~	room enough
tired and beat	

1. A: Where are you going on vacation this year?
   B: We're going to the mountains to be alone. We want to get away from the <u>hustling crowds</u>.
2. A: This project is _____. I don't think I can finish on time.
   B: Keep trying. I know you can do it!
3. A: I don't mind the bad weather. I love the air after it rains.
   B: Me, too. It smells so _____.
4. A: What a day! I worked from 8 A.M. until 10 P.M.
   B: You look _____. Can I get you something to eat and drink?
5. A: Please, sit here. There's _____ for two.
   B: Thank you.

RHYTHM and BLUES

Like jazz, rhythm and blues is a uniquely American form of music. **The Drifters** *started singing together in 1953 and continued to make hit records through the 1970s.*

Listening

2 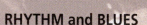 Listen to the song. Put the pictures in the correct order to tell the man's story.

3 🎧 **Listen to the song again. Fill in the blanks.**

Up on the Roof

When this old _____
starts getting me down

And people are just too much
for me to face,

I climb way up to the top of
the _____

And all my _____ just
drift right into space.

On the roof it's peaceful as
can be

And there the _____
below can't bother me.

Let me tell you now

When I come _____
feeling tired and beat,

I go up where the
_____ is fresh and
sweet.

I get away from the hustling
crowds

And all that rat-race noise
down in the _____.

On the roof's the only place I
know

Where you just have to wish
to make it so,

Let's go up on the roof.

At night the stars put on a
_____ for free,

And darling, you can share it
all with me.

I keep-a tellin' you

Right smack dab in the
middle of _____

I've found a _____
that's trouble proof.

And if this _____
starts getting you down,

There's room enough for two

Up on the roof,
Up on the roof.
Oh come on, baby
Oh come on, honey
Everything is all right . . .

4 *PAIRS.* **Compare your answers.**

Speaking

5 *GROUPS OF 3.* **Discuss the questions.**

Describe the character's mood. Why does he/she feel this way?
What is your idea of paradise? Describe it.

How sweet it is!

Vocabulary Food
Grammar Count and non-count nouns; *How much/How many*;
Quantifiers: *much, many, a lot of*
Speaking Talking about foods you like

Lesson A

Getting started

1 **PAIRS.** Match the photos with the words in the box.

bread ____   butter _A_   cake ____   candy ____   cheese ____

chocolate ____   coffee ____   cookies ____   crackers ____   fruit ____

ice cream ____   milk ____   nuts ____   potato chips ____   soda ____

2 🎧 Listen and check your answers. Then listen and repeat.

3 **PAIRS.** Which foods in Exercise 1 are sweet and which are not sweet?
Write them in the correct column.

Sweet	Not sweet
soda	cheese

Listening

4 **PAIRS.** Do you know what the following word and phrase mean: *chocoholic* and *to have a sweet tooth*?

5 🎧 Listen to the interview and check (✓) the words from Exercise 1 that you hear.

6 🎧 Listen again. Are the sentences true or false? Write *T* or *F* next to each one.

1. Lorraine eats some chocolate almost every day. T
2. Tae-Soon eats a lot of sweet things.
3. Gustavo eats a lot of cookies.
4. Gustavo buys a lot of potato chips.
5. Janice prefers salty food.

Reading

7 **PAIRS.** Do you think sweet foods are healthy or unhealthy for you? Read the article and compare your answers.

Short and Sweet
The Truth about Sweets

Are you crazy about sweets? How many cookies do you eat in a day? How much chocolate? How much soda do you drink? A lot of people love sweets. In fact, a lot of people eat and drink too many sweet things. And that's not good. It can lead to health problems.

If you eat a lot of cookies, ice cream, or cake—be careful. Doctors say that too many sweets are bad for your health. They say to eat a variety of foods: lots of fruits and vegetables, and smaller portions of bread, meat, and dairy. Then have a cookie or two for dessert.

Are two cookies enough to satisfy your sweet tooth? If not, try these suggestions: eat some fruit instead of a lot of chocolate or ice cream, drink some juice instead of soda, or eat a few nuts instead of some candy.

8 Read the article again. Underline the word that makes each sentence true.

1. A lot of people love **sweets / butter**.
2. Too many **cookies / vegetables** are bad for your health.
3. It's OK to eat one or two **cookies / cakes** for dessert.
4. It's good to eat some **fruit / chocolate** instead of ice cream.

13

Grammar focus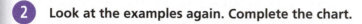

1   **Study the examples of count and non-count nouns.**

one cookie	**two** crackers	**five** nuts
some butter	**some** bread	**some** cheese

2   **Look at the examples again. Complete the chart.**

Count and non-count nouns

Count nouns are things that you can count separately.
For example: _cookie_ , _____ , _____

Non-count nouns are things that you can't count separately.
For example: _butter_ , _____ , _____

> *Grammar Reference page 145*

3   **Study the examples with the quantifiers *much, many,* and *a lot of.***

Do you eat **much** butter? No, **not much**.
I don't put **much** butter on my bread.
How **many** cookies do you eat? **Not many**.

I don't eat **many** sweets.
Our family eats **a lot of** potato chips.
We also eat **a lot of** fruit.

4   **Look at the examples again. Complete the rules with *much, many,* or *a lot of.***

Quantifiers: *much, many, a lot of*

Use _____ with count nouns in questions and negatives.

Use _____ with non-count nouns in questions and negatives.

Use _____ with count and non-count nouns in affirmative sentences.

> *Grammar Reference page 145*

5   **Underline the correct word or words in each sentence.**

1. A: How **much / many** fruit do you eat everyday?
   B: **A lot / Much / Many**. I really like fruit.
2. A: Do you drink **much / many** soda?
   B: No, not **much / many**, but I drink **a lot of / much / many** coffee.
3. A: Are there **much / many** cakes on the table?
   B: I don't know. There were **a lot / much / many** this morning.
4. A: Do you eat **much / many** sweets?
   B: Not **much / many**. I like salty things better.
5. A: There isn't **much / many** ice cream in the freezer.
   B: Really? Well, I bought **a lot / much / many** yesterday!

Pronunciation

6 🎧 Listen. Notice the vowel sounds of /ɑ/ in *not* and /ʌ/ in *nut*.

not	nut	one nut	not a lot
much	much butter	Do you eat much butter?	No, not much.
a lot	a lot of nuts	I eat a lot of nuts.	
love	love butter	How much butter do you eat?	A lot. I love butter!

7 🎧 Listen and repeat.

Speaking

8 *BEFORE YOU SPEAK.*
Complete the first column with the names of other foods and beverages.

9 *PAIRS.* Take turns. Interview each other. Use *much, many, or,* and *a lot of* in your questions and answers. Take notes.

A: Do you eat chocolate?
B: Yes.
A: How much chocolate do you eat in a week?
B: A lot—I eat some every day!

10 Does your partner have a sweet tooth? Report to the class.

Do you have a sweet tooth?

	Yes or No	How much/many _____ do you eat/drink in a week?
Sweet		
chocolate		
Not sweet		
coffee		

Writing

11 Dr. Food has a website about favorite foods. What do you like to eat? Write an email to Dr. Food about the foods you like and tell how much you eat.

CONVERSATION TO GO

A: Do you eat **much** chocolate?
B: Yes, **a lot**!

Job exchange

Vocabulary Job duties
Grammar Modal: *can* for ability
Speaking Asking about job skills

Lesson A

Getting started

1 **PAIRS.** Match the verbs in the box with the groups of nouns to create different job skills. Some verbs will be used more than one time.

design	drive	manage	read
repair	sing	~~type~~	write

1. _____type_____ 80 words a minute, a letter, a report
2. _____ a website, a building, a brochure
3. _____ a car, a photocopier, a computer
4. _____ a hotel, a project, people
5. _____ English, Portuguese, Spanish
   _____
6. _____ a car, a truck, a motorcycle
   _____
7. _____ a story, a report, a speech
   _____
8. _____ a song
   _____

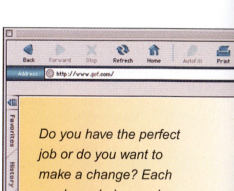

Do you have the perfect job or do you want to make a change? Each week, we help people decide on a new career. Try a new job for one week and decide if you want to make a change.

2 **Underline the correct verb to complete each sentence.**

1. I want to **design** / **repair** a website that's easy to use.
2. It's important to **read** / **drive** maps correctly in my job.
3. My job is to **repair** / **drive** a truck and deliver packages.
4. These actors also **speak** / **sing** and dance.
5. I need to **speak** / **type** Japanese to some of our guests.
6. Please call the service department to **repair** / **write** the copier.
7. Our assistant can **manage** / **type** 60 words a minute.
8. I **manage** /**design** a team of 20 employees.

Reading

3 **PAIRS.** Gary Hampton, a hotel manager, and Viviane Lisboa, a driver, are exchanging jobs. Predict the answers. Then read the text and check your answers.

1. _____ likes the new job.
2. _____ doesn't like the new job.

4 Read the text again and complete the sentences with *V* (Viviane), *G* (Gary), or *B* (both).

1. ____ can speak several languages.
2. ____ can drive a truck.
3. ____ can't read maps.
4. ____ can't sing.
5. ____ can't speak Japanese.

Changing Jobs: The Career Consultants

Viviane Lisboa is a driver with FedEx®. She delivers packages. But she wants to work around more people. This week she is exchanging jobs with Gary Hampton, a hotel manager from San Francisco. Can Viviane become the perfect hotel manager?

"This is basically the worst week of my life. Gary is really good with the guests. He can speak Japanese, Korean, and Spanish. We have a group of Japanese guests tonight, and I can't understand anything they say. I can only say *konnichi wa*, or *good day*. Tonight is also cabaret night with karaoke. Usually the manager does the first song. The problem is—I can't sing!"

Gary Hampton is a successful hotel manager from San Francisco. He wants to work outside in the fresh air and have a regular schedule. Can Gary become the perfect Fed Ex® driver?

"I love this job. I'm outside all day. I can drive a truck with no problem. But right now . . . I can't move! I'm stuck in traffic in the middle of the city. I can't keep my schedule like this. And I do have one problem. I can't read maps well—especially city maps! So, right now . . . I'm lost! But I really love this job!"

65

Grammar focus

1 **Study the examples with** *can* **for ability.**

> Gary **can drive** a car.
> Viviane **can't speak** Japanese.
> **Can** Gary **become** the perfect driver?
> Yes, he **can**. / No, he **can't**.

2 **Look at the examples again. Complete the chart.**

Modal: *can* for ability		
Affirmative statements	I/You/He/She/We/They	_____
Negative statements	I/You/He/She/We/They	_____ drive a truck.

NOTE: Always use the base form of the verb with *can* and *can't*.

Yes/No questions	Short answers
_____ you type?	Yes, I _____ .
	No, I _____ .

> *Grammar Reference page 145*

3 **Write questions and short answers with** *can or can't***.**

1. A: you / read / map?   Can you read a map?
   B: yes   Yes, I can.
2. A: she / drive / car?
   B: no
3. A: you / type / fast?
   B: yes
4. A: he / speak / French well?
   B: yes
5. A: they / finish / the report on time?
   B: no
6. A: Regina / read / Russian?
   B: yes
7. A: they / repair / all the computers?
   B: yes
8. A: you / design / websites?
   B: no

Pronunciation

4 🎧 **Listen.** Notice the weak and strong pronunciations of *can*. Notice the strong pronunciation of *can't*.

I can drive a truck.	I **can't** sing.
Can you read a map?	Yes, I **can**. / No, I **can't**.

5 🎧 **Listen again and repeat.**

6 🎧 **Listen and underline the word you hear.**

1. We **can / can't** repair computers.
2. I **can / can't** read a map.
3. He **can / can't** design websites.
4. She **can / can't** speak Spanish.
5. **Can / Can't** you sing?
6. I **can / can't** type fast.

Speaking

7 *PAIRS.* **Take turns interviewing each other.**

Can you use a computer? Can you type fast? Can you speak . . . ?

Can you . . . ?

Administration	Yes	No	Business	Yes	No
use a computer/type			manage a company		
speak a foreign language			write a business plan		
manage your time			manage other people		

Technology	Yes	No	Entertainment	Yes	No
write computer programs			dance		
design a website			sing		
repair a computer			play an instrument		

8 **Which type of job can your partner do? Does your partner agree with you?**

Writing

9 **Think about your job skills. Write about the skills you have and the skills you don't have now, but want to learn. Use *can* and *can't* and some of the vocabulary in this unit.**

CONVERSATION TO GO

A: **Can** you **read** a map?
B: **No**, I **can't**.

UNIT 15

Family

Vocabulary Family members
Grammar Present continuous for now
Speaking Talking about what people are doing at the moment

Lesson A

Getting started

1 **PAIRS.** Look at the Simpson family tree. Use words in the box to complete the sentences. You will not use one of the words.

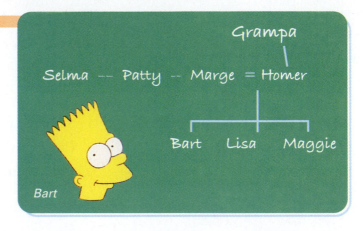

Grampa

Selma -- Patty -- Marge = Homer

Bart   Lisa   Maggie

Bart

aunts	brother	children	daughters	father
grandfather	grandmother	husband	mother	parents
sisters	son	uncles	~~wife~~	

Homer

1. Marge is my ___wife___.
2. We have three _____.
3. Maggie and Lisa are my _____.
4. Bart is my _____.
5. Grampa is my _____.

Marge

6. Homer is my _____.
7. I have two _____, Selma and Patty.

Maggie

8. Bart is my _____.
9. My _____ are Homer and Marge.
10. Marge is my _____.

Lisa

11. I have two _____, Selma and Patty.
12. My mother doesn't have any brothers, so I don't have any _____.
13. Grampa is my _____.

2 🎧 Listen to the riddles about different family members. Who is it? Write the family member next to each number.

1. ___uncle___   3. _____   5. _____

2. _____   4. _____   6. _____

68

3 ***PAIRS.*** Look at the example of the Simpson family tree. Draw your family tree. Then describe it to your partner.

Reading

4 ***PAIRS.*** Look at the picture. Which of the Simpsons is happy? Not happy? Read the letter to check your answers.

| Bart | Homer | Marge | Maggie | Lisa |

5 Read the letter again. Are the sentences true or false? Write *T* or *F* next to each one.

1. Bart is sitting in the kitchen. F
2. Bart doesn't like the TV program.
3. Homer wants to be with his friends.
4. Marge is happy because her sisters are visiting.
5. Marge's sisters are in her kitchen.
6. Maggie is watching Bart.
7. Lisa wants the family to talk to each other.

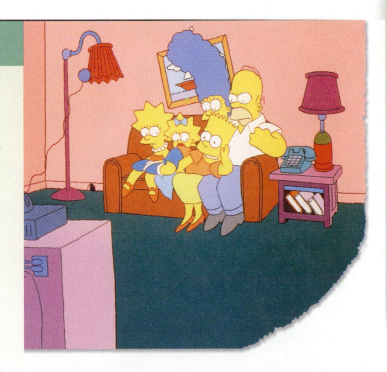

Readers' Letters

Your TV favorites . . .

My favorite Simpsons' program is *A Night at Home with the Family*. I love the moment when the family is sitting on the sofa together and they are watching TV. Bart is very happy because he's lying across everyone and he's watching his favorite program. But his parents and his sisters aren't so happy. In fact, they're not having much fun. Homer isn't happy because he isn't spending time with his friends. Marge isn't happy because her sisters are visiting and they're making a mess in her kitchen. Maggie isn't watching TV because she's looking at Bart. And Lisa...is she enjoying herself? No, she isn't. She's getting angry because the family isn't talking—they are just watching TV!   *C. Brown, Boston*

Grammar focus

1 **Study the examples of the present continuous.**

> I'm **watching** *The Simpsons*!
> Maggie **is looking** at Bart.
> Homer **isn't talking** to his friends.
>
> They're **sitting** on the sofa.
> They're **not spending** time with their friends.
> **Are** you **having fun**? Yes, **I am**. / No, **I'm not**.

2 **Look at the examples again. Complete the chart.**

Present continuous
Use the _____ to describe actions that people are doing now.
Use a form of the verb *be* + a verb that ends in _____.
Note the spelling:

watch ➔ watch**ing**	have ➔ hav**ing**	hit ➔ hit**ting**
visit ➔ _____	make ➔ _____	sit ➔ _____

> **Grammar Reference page 146**

3 🎧 **Listen and find out what the Cormack family is doing. Complete the sentences.**

1. Mr. Cormack _____is getting up_____.
2. His wife _____.
3. His son _____.
4. His daughter _____.
5. The children _____.

4 **Complete the sentences with the correct form of the present continuous. Use the verbs in parentheses.**

1. A: What ____are you doing____ ? (you/do)

   B: I ____'m cooking____ breakfast. (cook)

2. A: Where _____? (you/go)

   B: I _____ to work.

3. A: Who _____ to? (she/talk)

   B: She _____ to her mother.

4. A: What are they doing now?

   B: They _____ soccer. (play)

5. A: It's 7:00. _____ *The Simpsons*? (you/watch)

   B: No, I _____ a movie.

Pronunciation

5 🎧 **Listen. Notice the stressed words in these sentences.**

The **fam**ily is **sit**ting on the **so**fa.

What are they **do**ing?

Are they **hav**ing **fun**?

They **are**n't **talk**ing.

They're **watch**ing a **mov**ie.

Yes, they **are**.

6 🎧 **Listen again and repeat.**

7 *PAIRS.* **Practice the conversations in Exercise 4.**

Speaking

8 *PAIRS.* **Student A, look at page 137. Student B, look the picture of the Cormack family on this page. Take turns. Ask questions to find five differences between the two pictures. Take notes.**

A: Is the son listening to music?
B: No, he isn't. He's…

Writing

9 **What time is it right now? Think of five people you know. What are they probably doing right now? Write sentences about them. Use the present continuous.**

CONVERSATION TO GO

A: What**'s** your brother **doing** now?
B: He**'s doing** his homework.

In a café

Vocabulary Food and drink
Grammar Modals: *would like, will have,* and *can* for ordering
Speaking Ordering in a restaurant

Getting started

1 Look at the pictures of the food and beverages on page 73. Write the numbers of the pictures next to the correct items on the café menu.

2 *PAIRS.* Compare your answers.

Listening

3 🎧 Regina is calling to place a take-out order. Listen to her conversation and write the missing prices on the menu.

4 🎧 Listen to the rest of Regina's conversation. Underline the items that she orders.

1. a chicken sandwich with tomato / a cheese sandwich with tomato
2. a large coffee / a large milk
3. hot chocolate / chocolate cake

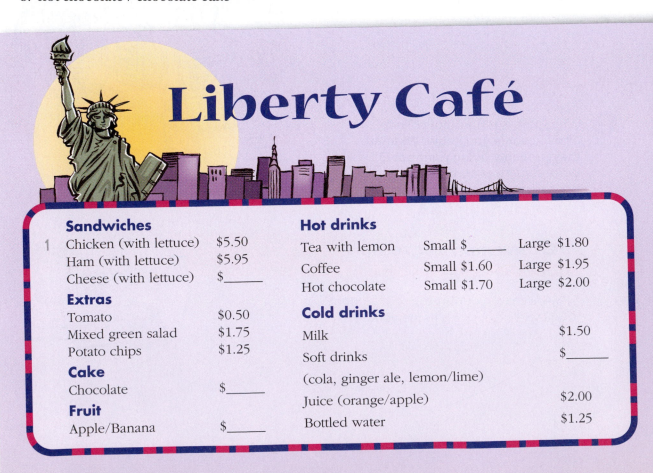

Liberty Café

Sandwiches			**Hot drinks**		
1 Chicken (with lettuce)	$5.50		Tea with lemon	Small $_____	Large $1.80
Ham (with lettuce)	$5.95		Coffee	Small $1.60	Large $1.95
Cheese (with lettuce)	$_____		Hot chocolate	Small $1.70	Large $2.00
Extras			**Cold drinks**		
Tomato	$0.50		Milk		$1.50
Mixed green salad	$1.75		Soft drinks		$_____
Potato chips	$1.25		(cola, ginger ale, lemon/lime)		
Cake			Juice (orange/apple)		$2.00
Chocolate	$_____		Bottled water		$1.25
Fruit					
Apple/Banana	$_____				

Pronunciation

5 🎧 **Listen. Notice the vowel sounds of /i/ in *tea* and /ɪ/ in *milk*.**

tea	milk	tea with milk	Tea with milk, please.
cheese	sandwich	a cheese sandwich	I'd like a cheese sandwich.
chicken	sandwich	a chicken sandwich	Can I have a chicken sandwich?
three	fifty	three-fifty	It's $3.50.

6 🎧 **Listen and repeat.**

7 *PAIRS.* **You each have $10. Tell each other what you want to eat and drink from the Liberty Café menu. Say how much it costs.**

I'd like a cheese sandwich with tomato, a small tea with lemon, and an apple. The total is $8.25.

Grammar focus

1 Study the examples. Notice the different ways to order in a restaurant.

> **I'd like** a small soft drink.
> **I'll have** bottled water, please.
> **Can I have** a house salad?

2 Look at the examples again. Complete the explanation in the chart.

Modals: *would like, will have,* and *can* for ordering
_____, _____, and _____ are all polite ways to say *I want* when you order food in a restaurant.

Grammar Reference page 146

3 Complete the conversations. There may be more than one correct answer.

1. A: Are you ready to order?

   B: Yes, _____ a chicken, lettuce, and tomato sandwich.
   And _____ potato chips with that, please.

   A: Anything else?

   B: Yes, _____ a small orange juice, please?

2. A: Can I take your order?

   B: Yes, _____ tea with lemon to go?

   A: Small or large?

   B: Large, please.

   A: Is that all?

   B: No, _____ a piece of banana cake, please.

3. A: Good morning.

   B: Good morning. _____ a coffee with milk.
   Make it a large.

   A: Yes, here you are.

   B: And _____ an apple, please. How much is that?

4 **PAIRS.** Compare your answers. Then practice the conversations in Exercise 3.

Speaking

5 **GROUPS OF 3.** Student A, you are a waiter/waitress in a café. Students B and C, you are customers.

Student A, look at page 138. Students B and C, look at the menu on this page and decide what you want to have. Give your order to the waiter/waitress.

A: Can I take your order?
B: Yes, I'd like a cheese and tomato sandwich.
C: I'll have a ham sandwich. Can I have a house salad with that, please?

Lunch Munchies

SANDWICHES		BEVERAGES		
			Small	Large
Ham and cheese	$5.25			
Chicken, lettuce, and tomato	$5.75	Juice	$1.50	$1.80
Cheese and tomato	$4.65	*(orange, apple, tomato)*		
		Soft drinks	$1.10	$1.40
SIDES		*(cola, lemon/lime, ginger ale)*		
Potato chips	$1.25			
House salad	$2.25	Bottled water		$1.35
Fruit salad	$3.00	Coffee	$1.00	$1.35
		Tea	$1.00	$1.35
CAKES				
Chocolate, banana, lemon	$1.95	Hot chocolate	$1.20	$1.55

Writing

6 You're planning a party. Choose the menu from Liberty Café or Lunch Munchies. Write an email to the café manager. Tell what food and drinks you'd like at the party. Also, ask for some food or drink items not on the menu. Use *would like* and *can* and some of the vocabulary from this unit.

CONVERSATION TO GO

A: **Can** I **take** your order?
B: **I'd like** a large cup of coffee, please.

75

Unit 13 How sweet it is!

1 🎧 Listen to the model conversation. Look at the photos and the chart.

2 *PAIRS.* Student A, you want to improve your eating habits. Student B, you are a nutritionist. Ask questions to find out about Student A's eating habits. Then make some recommendations.

Client name: _____Antonio_____	Client name: _____
Recommendations:	Recommendations:
Eat more fruit.	_____
Drink water.	_____
_____	_____
_____	_____
_____	_____

Unit 14 Job exchange

3 Look at the list of abilities and write two more.

4 🎧 Listen to the model conversation and look at the list of abilities.

5 *CLASS.* Walk around the room and ask questions. Find someone who . . .

Name	Job skills	Name	Other skills
_____	can design a website.	_____	can speak three languages.
_____	can drive a truck.	_____	can ride a bicycle.
_____	can write computer programs.	_____	can play an instrument.
_____	can _____.	_____	can _____.

Unit 15 Family

6 🎧 Listen to the model conversation and look at the picture.

7 *2 PAIRS.* Team 1 (Students A and C) and Team 2 (Students B and D). Students A and B, look at page 140. Students C and D look at the picture of the Santos family on this page.

8 Teams take turns. Student C ask Student A what one of the Santos family members is doing. Student A act out what the family member is doing. Student C guess. Student A can only give two pantomime clues. Each correct sentence receives one point. Keep score.

Uncle   Aunt   Grandfather   Grandmother   Father   Mother   Daughter   Son

Unit 16 In a café

9 🎧 Listen to the model conversation.

10 *2 PAIRS.* You are in a café. Students A and B look at the menu on page 140. You are the customers.

11 Students C and D, you are both waiters/waitresses. Student C, take Student A's order. You can't write anything down. At the end of the order, you must repeat everything Student A ordered. Each item you remember correctly receives one point. Subtract a point for each item you forget. Then Student D, take your turn and take a different order from Student B.

12 Who remembered the most?

Hurricane

Vocabulary Weather; seasons; clothes
Grammar Action and non-action verbs
Speaking Comparing usual and current situations

Getting started

1 **PAIRS.** **Describe the season in each picture. Choose one sentence from each column.**

It's spring. It's 70 degrees. It's warm. It's windy.

It's 90° F.	It's really cold.	It's raining.
It's 32° F.	It's really hot.	It's snowing.
It's 70° F.	It's warm.	It's sunny
It's 50° F.	It's cool.	It's windy.

spring

autumn

summer

winter

2 **Match the words with the clothes in the pictures.**

boots _____	gloves _____	hat _____	jacket _____
raincoat _____	sandals _____	scarf _____	shorts _____
sun hat _____	T-shirt _____	sweater __A__	umbrella _____

Pronunciation

3 🎧 **Listen. Notice the groups of consonant sounds in these words.**

scarf	**gl**oves	I need my **sc**arf and **gl**oves.
it's	co**ld**	**It's** co**ld**.
spring	**sn**owing	**It's spr**ing, but **it's sn**owing.
sixty-**three**	**degr**ees	**It's** sixty-**three degr**ees.

4 🎧 **Listen and repeat.**

5 *GROUPS OF 3.* **Answer these questions about the weather where you live.**

What are the seasons like where you live? Describe them.
What types of clothes do you wear each season?
Do you like the weather there? Why or why not?

Listening

6 **Pairs. Guess. Which three of these places often have hurricanes? See page 141 for the answers.**

Arizona	Canada	Colorado
Florida	Jamaica	Mexico

7 🎧 **Listen to the news report about a dangerous hurricane. Check (✓) the weather conditions you hear.**

1. It's 73°. ____
   It's 63°. ____

2. It's cold and windy. ____
   It's warm and windy. ____

3. It's raining. ____
   It's sunny. ____

8 🎧 **Listen to the news report again. Are the sentences true or false? Write *T* or *F* next to each one.**

1. The hurricane's name is Charlie. T
2. The hurricane is in Miami now.
3. They know this hurricane is a big one.
4. Many people are leaving.
5. Some people are trying to protect their homes.
6. People are carrying umbrellas.
7. Miami has several hurricanes in a season.

17

Grammar focus

1 Look at the examples of action and non-action verbs.
Write *A* next to the sentences with action verbs. Write
NA next to the sentences with non-action verbs.

> We **know** this for a fact.
> They**'re covering** windows.
> A lot of people **are leaving**.
> We**'re** all **wearing** raincoats and hats.
> Of course, some people **prefer** to stay.
> I **need** some dry clothes!
> Other people **are packing**.
> People **like** to live in Miami.

2 Look at the examples again. Circle the correct words to
complete the explanations.

> **Action versus non-action verbs**
>
> **Action verbs / non-action verbs** (like *be, understand, have,* and *love*) describe states
> or situations.
>
> **Action verbs / non-action verbs** are not usually used in the present continuous.

> *Grammar Reference page 146*

3 Complete the sentences with the correct form of the verb in parentheses.
Use the simple present or present continuous.

1. In London, it's usually cold in February and it ___rains___ a lot. (rain) It's very cold
   today and it _____ (snow).

2. Today is the first day of spring, and all of Paris _____ (look) beautiful. The sun
   _____ (shine), and it's about 60 degrees. People _____ (wear) sweaters
   and jackets. The trees _____ (turn) green and the birds _____ (sing).

3. In Seattle it _____ (rain) a lot all year. Sometimes they _____ (have) hot,
   sunny weather in July and August with temperatures above 90 degrees. Today it
   _____ (rain) and everyone _____ (carry) umbrellas.

4. Autumn in Rome is beautiful. The average temperature in October is about 55
   degrees. Today, the sun _____ (not shine) but at least it _____ (not rain).

Speaking

4 **BEFORE YOU SPEAK.** Think of your favorite season. Choose a day in that season (for example, *Spring, April 28*). Imagine the weather. Imagine what you and other people are wearing and doing. Take notes.

Date: _____

Season: _____

Weather: _____

Clothes: _____

Activities: _____

5 **GROUPS OF 3.** Take turns. Describe the day you're imagining.

Today is April 28th. The weather is perfect. It's 70 degrees, and I'm wearing . . .

6 Tell the class about one of your partners' days.

Writing

7 An American friend is coming to your country for a year. Your friend sends you an email and wants to know about the weather. Write an email with helpful information.

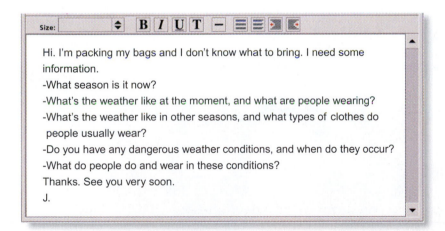

| Size: ⬦ | **B** | *I* | **U** | T | — | ≡ | ≡ | ≡ | ≣ |

Hi. I'm packing my bags and I don't know what to bring. I need some information.
-What season is it now?
-What's the weather like at the moment, and what are people wearing?
-What's the weather like in other seasons, and what types of clothes do people usually wear?
-Do you have any dangerous weather conditions, and when do they occur?
-What do people do and wear in these conditions?
Thanks. See you very soon.
J.

CONVERSATION TO GO

A: What's the weather like?
B: The sun **is shining**. It **doesn't** always **rain** in Seattle.

Memories

Vocabulary Memorable, people, events, and possessions
Grammar *be* simple past
Speaking Talking about memories

Lesson A

Getting started

1 Think about memorable people, events, and possessions in your life. Write two for each circle.

my great-grandmother

People

Possessions

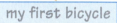

my first bicycle

Events

my 16th birthday

2 **PAIRS.** Choose one person, event, and possession. Why do you remember them?

3 Use the words and phrases in the box to complete the questions.
Use each word or phrase once.

How	How many	How much	What
When	Where	Who	

1. <u>How many</u> telephone numbers can you remember?
2. _____ is your mother's birthday?
3. _____ is your best friend's telephone number?
4. _____ old is your father?
5. _____ are the actors in your favorite TV show?
6. _____ is your passport or identification card now?
7. _____ does a ticket to the movies cost?

Listening

4 🎧 Listen to two friends, Rosa and Man–Ho, play the memory game. Check (✓) the memories they talk about.

Best vacation _____

Best friend at school _____

First girlfriend _____

First boyfriend _____

5 🎧 Listen again. Underline the answers they give to the questions.

Rosa:
Miami last year / Mexico three years ago
family vacation / family visit
a lot to do / not much to do
a lot of kids her age / not many kids her age

Man–Ho:
Pretty and nice / beautiful and smart
British / Irish
15 and 16 / 16 and 18

18

Grammar focus

1 **Study the examples of the verb *be* in the simple past.**

> It **wasn't** a problem.
> How old **were** you? I **was** seventeen.
> Where **was** your best vacation? It **was** in Mexico.
> **Were** they the same age? Yes, they **were**. / No, they **weren't**.

2 **Look at the examples again. Complete the charts.**

be simple past: statements					
I/He/She/It	<u>was</u> (+)	young.	We/You/They	____ (+)	happy.
There	____ (–)	a lot to do.	There	____ (–)	any beaches.

be simple past: questions			
_____ it crowded?	Yes, it _____.	How old _____ you?	
_____ they late?	No, they _____.	When _____ she in Mexico?	

> **Grammar Reference page 146**

3 **Complete the conversations with the simple past of *be*.**

1. A: <u>Was</u> it a good vacation?

   B: No, it <u>wasn't</u> .

   A: Why?

   B: It <u>was</u> cloudy and cold all week!

2. A: When _____ the first World Cup soccer match?

   B: It _____ in 1930.

   A: _____ it in Greece?

   B: No, it _____. It _____ in Uruguay.

3. A: Where _____ the summer Olympic Games in 2000?

   B: They _____ in Sydney, Australia.

   A: How many different sports _____ there?

   B: There _____ 37, I think.

Pronunciation

4 🎧 **Listen. Notice the different weak and strong pronunciations of *was* and *were* and the strong pronunciations of *wasn't* and *weren't*.**

How old were you? I was seventeen.

There **weren't** many people. It **wasn't** a problem.

Was it a good vacation? Yes, it **was**.

Were the beaches nice? Yes, they **were**.

5 🎧 **Listen again and repeat.**

Speaking

6 *GROUPS OF 3.* **Take turns. Toss a coin (one side of the coin = move one space, the other side = move two spaces). When you land on a space, your classmates will use use the cue to ask you a question. If your sentence is correct, stay on the space. If it is incorrect, move back to where you started your turn. The first person to reach FINISH wins.**

B: *Where was your best vacation?*
A: *It was in Mexico.*
C: *Who were you with?*
A: *I was with my family. We . . .*

Writing

7 **Think about a memorable person, possession, or event in your life. Write a paragraph describing the person or thing. Explain why he, she, or it is memorable. Use the simple past of the verb** *be.*

> ### CONVERSATION TO GO
>
> A: What **was** your favorite subject in school?
> B: Well, it **wasn't** English or math. It **was** gym class!

A day in the life of…

Vocabulary Everyday activities
Grammar Simple past: regular verbs (affirmative and negative)
Speaking Talking about your day

Lesson A

Getting started

1 Use the verbs in the box to complete the sentences about Kate Childers' typical day.

arrive	call	close	decide	finish	open
relax	reply	~~start~~	want	watch	

1. I _start_ each day with a strong cup of coffee.

2. I _____ the morning news on TV.

3. I listen to the weather report so I can _____ what to wear.

4. I work out at the gym for an hour because I _____ to stay in shape.

5. I meet friends for lunch and _____ a bit.

6. I _____ lunch by 2:30 so I can be at work by 3:00.

7. I check my voice mail and _____ people back.

8. Then I look at my email and _____ to messages.

9. Most members of the theater staff _____ at 4:00.

10. The theater doors _____ at 7:00.

11. We usually _____ the doors at 10:30, and I go home at 11:00.

2 **PAIRS.** Describe a typical day for you. Use some of the verbs in Exercise 1.

I arrive at the office at 9:00 A.M. First, I read my emails and reply to them.

86

Reading

3 **Read the article and answer the question.**

How is Kate Childers' day in the article different from her typical day at work?

4 **Read the article again. Are the sentences true or false? Write *T* or *F* next to each one.**

1. The show that Kate organized started in the morning. F
2. She talked to MTV in the afternoon.
3. The new dressing room assistant started work at 5:00 P.M.
4. Kate talked to many people at the Awards show.
5. Kate finished work in the early evening.

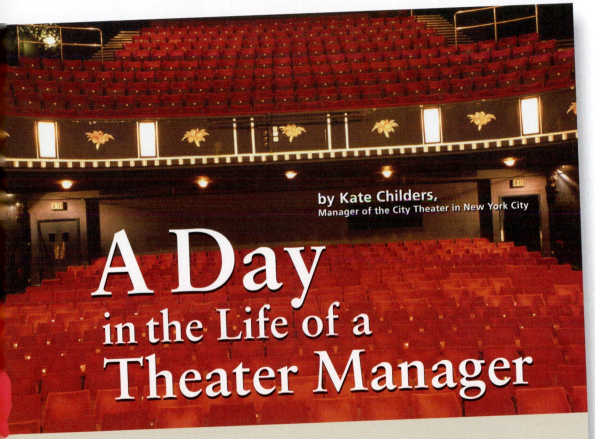

by **Kate Childers,**
Manager of the City Theater in New York City

A Day
in the Life of a
Theater Manager

The MTV Music Awards are today. It's now noon— my workday started early. This morning I wanted to be in the office by 9:00. I decided to eat breakfast at my desk. I watched some entertainment news on TV— about the MTV Music Awards, of course! Then the phone started ringing.

Now it's 4:00 P.M. A busy afternoon. Mostly I talked on the phone! I called MTV about last-minute details for the program. I asked the organizers about the number of special guests. Then I talked to the manager of the Raffles Agency in Manhattan about the new dressing room assistant.

It's 3:00 A.M.— the next day! I'm so tired! Imogen, the new dressing room assistant, didn't arrive until 5:00 P.M. The Awards started at 7:30. I didn't talk to a lot of people because I was so busy. I didn't even watch the program! But I think everyone loved it! Imogen and I finished work a few minutes ago. It's time to go home and relax.

Welcome to the life of a theater manager!

Grammar focus

1 **Study the examples of the verbs in the simple past tense.**

> I call**ed** New York.
> The new assistant arriv**ed**.
> She **didn't watch** the program.
> We **didn't finish** with work until the next morning.

2 **Look at the examples again. Complete the chart.**

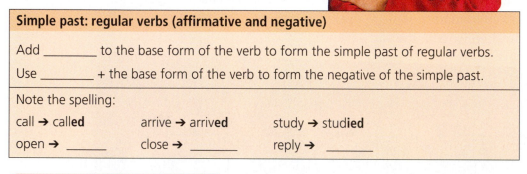

Simple past: regular verbs (affirmative and negative)
Add _____ to the base form of the verb to form the simple past of regular verbs.
Use _____ + the base form of the verb to form the negative of the simple past.
Note the spelling:

call ➔ call**ed**	arrive ➔ arriv**ed**	study ➔ stud**ied**
open ➔ _____	close ➔ _____	reply ➔ _____

> **Grammar Reference page 147**

3 **Look at Kate's "To Do" lists for the morning and the evening. Write complete sentences about which things she did or didn't do.**

To Do List:

Morning

cook breakfast **X**
call mother ✓
work out at gym **X**
watch entertainment news on TV ✓
look at new work schedule ✓

Evening

return to work at 6:00 P.M. ✓
check new concert posters **X**
talk to musicians ✓
plan schedule for next day **X**
finish paperwork ✓

1. _She didn't cook breakfast._
2. _She called her mother._
3. _____
4. _____
5. _____
6. _____
7. _____
8. _____
9. _____
10. _____

Pronunciation

4 🎧 Listen. Notice the three different pronunciations of the –*ed* ending in simple past verbs.

started /ɪd/	arrived /d/	talked /t/
	called	

5 🎧 Listen to more simple past verbs. Notice the pronunciation of the –*ed* ending. Write each verb in the correct sound group.

6 🎧 Listen and check your answers. Then listen again and repeat

Speaking

7 **BEFORE YOU SPEAK.** Write your "To Do" list for the past week. Write four things you did and four things you didn't do. Write ✓ next to things you did and *X* next to things you didn't do.

8 **GROUPS OF 4.** Exchange lists. Take turns. Say what the person did or didn't do last week.

Rei didn't start her new exercise class. She studied for her English test . . .

9 Is there one thing you all *did* last week? Is there one thing you all *didn't* do last week?

"To Do" list   week of / / /

start new exercise class X
study for English test ✓
_____
_____
_____
_____
_____
_____
_____

Writing

10 Write a paragraph describing what you did and didn't do last week. Use the past tense and some of the vocabulary from this unit.

CONVERSATION TO GO

A: You **watched** TV all weekend?
B: No, I **didn't**. I **studied** English.

UNIT 20

Love at first sight

Vocabulary Common irregular verbs
Grammar Simple past: irregular verbs
Speaking Telling a story

Lesson A

Getting started

1 Write the letter of the picture that matches each phrase. Two of the phrases match more than one picture.

buy her flowers _____C_____

fall in love _____ and _____

give presents _____

go to her house _____

leave her house _____

meet someone _____ and _____

say no _____

see him with her _____

2 *PAIRS.* Compare your answers.

(A) _____

(B) _____

(C) _____

90

Listening

3 **GROUPS OF 3.** Number the pictures to tell a story.
There are many possible variations.

4 🎧 Listen to the real-life love story of Jack, Debbie, and Cara.
Number the pictures according to the story you hear.

A_____ B_____ C_____ D_____ E_1_ F_____ G_____ H_____

5 🎧 Listen again and check your answers.

6 Compare your story with Jack, Debbie, and Cara's.
Are the stories the same or different?

F _____

D _____

G _____

E _____

H _____

Grammar focus

1 🎧 Listen again to Jack, Debbie, and Cara's love story. Write the irregular simple past of the verbs in the chart. Complete the rule.

Simple past: irregular verbs

meet __met__	give _____	fall _____
be __was__	say _____	know _____
go _____	leave _____	see _____
buy _____	think _____	come _____

Use *didn't* + the _____ form of the verb to make negative statements in the simple past.

Grammar Reference page 147

2 Use the correct form of the verbs in the box to complete the story. You will use some of the verbs more than one time.

be	fall	give	go	leave
meet	not love	say	see	think

Violet **(1)** _went_ on vacation to Italy. She **(2)** _____ a waiter

named Giovanni at a local restaurant and she **(3)** _____ in love

instantly. He **(4)** _____ very romantic and **(5)** _____ her flowers.

He **(6)** _____ that he loved her. Violet **(7)** _____ home two weeks later,

but Giovanni didn't go with her. She **(8)** _____ about him every

day. One month later she **(9)** _____ again for Italy. She **(10)** _____

to the restaurant and **(11)** _____ Giovanni with another woman.

She knew then that he **(12)** _____ her.

Pronunciation

3 🎧 **Listen. Notice the vowel sounds in of /eɪ/ in *came* and /ɛ/ in *went*.**

met	they met	They met, and he fell in love.
went	every day	He went to her house every day.
gave	expensive presents	He gave her expensive presents.
came	very upset	He came home very upset.

4 🎧 **Listen and repeat.**

Speaking

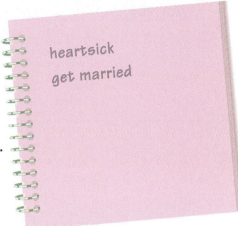

heartsick

get married

5 *BEFORE YOU SPEAK.* **Think about the story of Jack, Debbie, and Cara on page 91. Think of how to continue the story. What happened to them? Write some key words.**

Debbie was heartsick. She . . .

6 *PAIRS.* **Take turns. Tell the story with your new ideas. Are your stories the same or different?**

Writing

7 **Rewrite the story of Jack, Debbie, and Cara so that something is different. (For example, *They met again 10 years later . . .* or *The women are sisters . . .*) Use the simple past tense and some of the vocabulary from this unit.**

CONVERSATION TO GO

A: I **met** him in the supermarket.
B: We **fell** in love at first sight.

Unit 17 Hurricane

1 🎧 Listen to the model conversation and look at the words in the chart.

Temperature	Weather		Season	Clothes		
-5°F/-21°C	sunny	really hot	fall	shorts	sweater	hat
70°F/21°C	windy	cool	winter	sandals	gloves	T-shirt
90°F/32°C	raining	warm	spring	jacket	scarf	
50°F/10°C	snowing	really cold	summer	raincoat	boots	

2 *GROUPS OF 3.* Create a story. Take turns choosing information from each column and making a sentence with it. Decide as a group what the final sentence of the story will be. Create a few stories.

3 Tell your best story to the class.

Unit 18 Memories

4 🎧 Listen to the model conversation and look at the game.

5 *TWO PAIRS.* Take turns. Toss a coin (one side of the coin = move one space, the other side = move two spaces). When you land on a space, use the cue to ask your partner a question. Your partner answers the question. If your question and answer are correct, stay on the space. If they are incorrect, move back to where you started your turn. The first pair to reach FINISH wins.

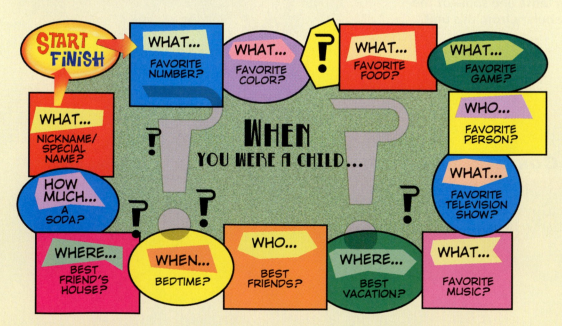

Unit 19 A day in the life of . . .

6 🎧 Listen to the model conversation.

7 **PAIRS.** Student A, look at Talia's daily planner on page 141. Student B, look at Talia's planner on this page.

Student A, say a sentence with the time and something Talia did. Student B, say what Talia didn't do at that time. Then Student B, say a sentence with the time and something Talia didn't do. Student A, say what Talia did do at that time. Take turns saying what Talia did and didn't do.

DAILY PLANNER			
Thursday		**Friday**	
8:00	stay in bed ✓	8:00	call the office ✗
9:00	watch the news ✗	9:00	study for banking test ✓
10:00	call the office ✗	10:00	clean house ✗
11:00	call Jane ✓		
12:00	talk to Simon ✗		
5:00	start dinner ✗	5:00	go shopping ✗
6:00		6:00	
7:00	watch TV ✓	7:00	ask John for help ✓
8:00		8:00	
9:00		9:00	dance all night ✓

Unit 20 Love at first sight

8 🎧 Listen to the model conversation and look at the pictures.

9 **GROUPS OF 3.** Take turns giving information to create a story about the woman and the man in the pictures. Use the simple past tense of the irregular verbs in the box and other verbs you know.

| be | buy | come | fall | give | go | leave | meet | say | see | think |

10 Tell your story to the class.

95

World of Music 3

Tom's Diner
Suzanne Vega

Vocabulary

1 **PAIRS.** Match the phrases in the box with the photos.

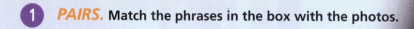

bells of the cathedral	diner on the corner	looking inside
~~pouring coffee~~	reading the newspaper	shaking an umbrella

A. _pouring coffee_   B. _____   C. _____

D. _____   E. _____   F. _____

Listening

2 🎧 Listen to the song. Put the photos in Exercise 1 in the correct order.

1. _____   2. _____   3. _____

4. _____   5. _____   6. _____

3 🎧 **Listen to the song again. Fill in the blanks.**

Tom's Diner

I _____ in the morning at the diner on the corner.

I _____ at the counter for the man to pour the coffee.

And he fills it only halfway, and before I even argue

He _____ out the window at somebody coming in.

"It is always nice to see you" says the man behind the counter

To the woman who has come in. She _____ her umbrella

And I look the other way as they _____ their hellos

I _____ not to see them

Instead I pour the milk.

I open up the paper, there's a story of an actor

Who had died while he was drinking. It was no one I had heard of.

And I _____ to the horoscope and _____ for the funnies

When I _____ someone watching me and so I raise my head.

There's a woman on the outside looking inside; does she see me?

No she does not really see me 'cause she sees her own reflection.

And I _____ not to notice that she's hitching up her skirt,

And while she _____ her stockings her hair _____ wet.

Oh, this rain it will continue through the morning

As I _____ to the bells of the cathedral, I _____ of your voice . . .

4 *PAIRS.* **Check your answers.**

Speaking

5 *GROUPS OF 3.* **Discuss these questions.**

Is the person telling the story a woman or a man? Is he/she alone or with someone? How do you know?

Why is the main character watching everyone? What are some of the things he/she notices?

Life and times

Vocabulary Important life events
Grammar Simple past: questions
Speaking Asking questions

Getting started

1 *PAIRS.* **Look at the photo. Who is this actress? Tell your partner what you know about her.**

2 Match the verbs in the box with the words and phrases to describe different life events.

be	become	get		go	have
make	move	start/finish	take		

1. __be__ born, an actress, 30 years old

2. _____ an English class, an exam, a driving test

3. _____ a film, a career change, money

4. _____ engaged, married, divorced

5. _____ to college, on vacation, on your honeymoon

6. _____ school, college, work

7. _____ to a house, to an apartment, to the U.S.

8. _____ famous, an engineer, an actress

9. _____ a son, children, a baby

3 *PAIRS.* **Tell each other true past events in your life. Use the vocabulary in Exercise 2.**

I was born in 1984.
I got married last year.

All About...
Julia
Roberts

STAR INTERVIEW

⭐ **Why is she famous?**
She's an American actress who starred in *Pretty Woman*, *My Best Friend's Wedding*, *Notting Hill*, *Erin Brockovich*, and *Mona Lisa Smile*.

⭐ **When was she born?**
Julia was born in 1967 in Georgia (U.S.).

⭐ **Did she always want to be an actress?**
No, she didn't. She wanted to work with animals.

⭐ **So, did she go to acting school?**
Yes, she did. She finished high school when she was 17 and started drama school.

⭐ **When did she get her first job?**
In 1984 she left her home and moved to New York. She got a job as a model for Click modeling agency.

⭐ **What about love? Is there someone special in her life?**
Julia was engaged to the actor Kiefer Sutherland, but they broke up just before the wedding in 1991. She got married to Lyle Lovett, a singer/actor, in 1993, but, sadly, it didn't work out. They got divorced two years later. She dated Benjamin Bratt, another TV and film actor, for several years.

⭐ **Did she get married again?**
In 2002, Julia got married again, this time to cameraman Daniel Moder. The wedding was near her home in New Mexico.

⭐ **When did she make her first film?**
She acted in her first film, *Blood Red*, with her brother, Eric, in 1986. She got her first Oscar nomination when she was 22 years old for *Steel Magnolias*.

⭐ **Did she ever win an Oscar?**
Yes, she did. She won an Oscar for Best Actress in *Erin Brockovich* in 2001. The movie was a big hit.

Reading

4 Read the article and fill in the year.

1967	She was born.
_____	She moved to New York.
_____	She made her first film.
_____	She got her first Oscar nomination.
_____	She got married to Lyle Lovett.
_____	She got divorced.
_____	She won the Oscar for Best Actress.
_____	She got married to Daniel Moder.

5 Read the article again. Are the statements true or false? Write *T* or *F* next to each one. Correct the statements that are false.

1. Julia Roberts is an American singer. F
   Julia Roberts is an American actress.

2. Julia Roberts starred in *Pretty Woman* and *Notting Hill*.

3. She wanted to teach English.

4. When Julia finished high school, she started acting school.

5 She was a model in New York.

6. Julia and her sister acted in the movie *Blood Red*.

7. She won an Oscar for *My Best Friend's Wedding*.

6 *PAIRS.* Check your answers.

Grammar focus

1 Study the examples of simple past tense questions.

> **Did** she always **want** to be an actress? No, she **didn't**.
> **Who did** she **act** with in her first film? Her brother.
> **Where did** she **move** to in 1984? New York.
> **When did** she **make** the film *Notting Hill?* In 1999.

2 Look at the examples again. Complete the questions in the chart.

Simple past: questions	
Did she always want to be an actress?	No, she **didn't**.
_____ she go to acting school?	Yes, she **did**.
When _____ she get her first job?	In 1984.
Where _____ she move to in 1984?	New York.
Who _____ she marry in 1993?	Lyle Lovett.
What _____ she win in 2001?	An Oscar for Best Actress.

Grammar Reference page 147

3 Read the answers. Then write the questions.

1. A: When _did Julia Roberts become an actress_?
   B: She became an actress at age 17.

2. A: Who _____
   for as a model?
   B: She worked for Click modeling agency.

3. A: _____?
   B: No, she didn't go to college.

4. A: When _____?
   B: She moved to New York in 1984

5. A: When _____
   to Lyle Lovett?
   B: She got married to Lyle Lovett in 1993.

6. A: When _____?
   B: They got divorced in 1995.

7. A: When _____?
   B: She won an Oscar in 2001.

8. A: Where _____?
   B: Julia and Daniel got married in New Mexico.

Pronunciation

4 🎧 Listen to these questions. Notice the weak pronunciation of *did* and the pronouns and the way these words are linked together.

Did she win an Oscar?   Did he grow up in New York?
When did she finish school? Who did he marry?
Where did she move to?   When did he make a movie?

5 🎧 Listen again and repeat.

All About...
Marc Anthony

His early life

Marc Anthony was born in 1969. His parents were from Puerto Rico, but he grew up in _New York City_. When he was a child, he loved _____.

His career

Marc Anthony had his first Spanish hit in the year 1993. His popularity started to grow. He sang _____ with Jennifer Lopez in 1998. The next year was a big year for Marc Anthony. In 1999, he won _____, he made a movie, and he made his first English album.

His personal life

But important things happened in 2000 also: That year Marc Anthony made an ad for milk. He got married to _____. Marc Anthony and his wife had difficult times in 2002. In July they _____, but six months later they were together again and they had a second wedding ceremony in San Juan!

Speaking

6 *PAIRS.* Take turns asking and answering questions to complete Marc Anthony's biography. Student A, look at page 138. Student B, look at this page.

B: *Where did he grow up?*
A: *He grew up in New York City.*

7 🎧 Now listen to Marc Anthony's biggest hit in English, "I Need to Know."

Writing

8 Choose a friend or family member. Write an "All about …" article like the one about Julia Roberts. Include questions in the simple past.

CONVERSATION TO GO

A: **When did** you **change** careers?
B: In 1997, 1999, 2001, and 2003!

It's on the right.

Vocabulary Parts of a building; ordinal numbers 1st – 10th
Grammar Imperatives; directions and prepositions of movement
Speaking Asking for and giving directions

Lesson A

Getting started

1. *PAIRS.* **Label the places on the hotel floor plan with the words in the box.**

business center	meeting rooms
café	parking garage
cash machine	reception desk
elevator	restaurant
fitness center	restrooms
gift shop	stairs
hallway	swimming pool
lobby	

2. 🎧 **Listen and check your answers.**

Pronunciation

3. 🎧 **Listen to these compound nouns from Exercise 1. Notice the main stress.**

swimming pool   restrooms

reception desk   business center

4. 🎧 **Now mark the main stress in these compound nouns.**

parking garage   gift shop

hallway   meeting rooms

fitness center   cash machine

5. *PAIRS.* **Compare your answers.**

6. 🎧 **Listen and repeat.**

102

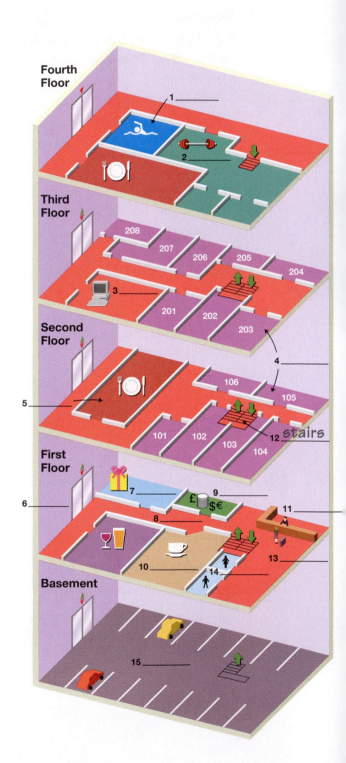

Fourth Floor

Third Floor

208 207 206 205 204
3
201 202 203

Second Floor

106
5
105
101 102 103 104
12 stairs

First Floor

7
9
6
8
11
10
13
14

Basement

15

Listening

7 🎧 **Listen to the conversations and circle the ordinal numbers you hear.**

| first | second | third | fourth | fifth |
| sixth | seventh | eighth | ninth | tenth |

8 🎧 **Listen to the numbers and repeat.**

9 *PAIRS.* **Look at the floor plan on page 102. Test your partner.**

Note: *in* the lobby, *in* the basement, *on* the first floor, *on* the second floor

A: *Where's the café?*
B: *It's on the first floor.*
A: *Correct.*

Grammar focus

10 **Study the examples of affirmative and negative imperative verbs.**

Go down the hallway.	**Don't go** to the second floor.
Take the elevator to the fourth floor.	**Don't take** the stairs.

11 **Look at the examples again. Complete the chart.**

Imperatives: affirmative and negative

The imperative form is the same as the _____ form of the verb.

Use _____ with the imperative to make the negative imperative.

> Grammar Reference page 147

12 **Complete the sentences with the imperative form.**

1. A: Are you ready?

   B: No. I need five more minutes. ___Wait___ for me in the lobby.

2. A: How do I get to the fitness center?

   B: _____ the elevator to the fourth floor.

3. A: Is there a cash machine in the lobby?

   B: Yes. _____ straight down this hallway. It's on the right.

4. A: Do you know anything about the new restaurant on Park Avenue?

   B: _____ to that restaurant! It's very expensive, and the food isn't very good.

Lesson B

Listening

1 🎧 Look at the floor plan on page 102. Listen to the hotel receptionist give directions. Follow the directions on the hotel floor plan and check (✓) the different places you hear.

2 🎧 Look at the floor plan on page 102. Listen again and follow the receptionist's directions. Where does the guest want to go?

Grammar focus

3 Match the following expressions for giving directions with the pictures.

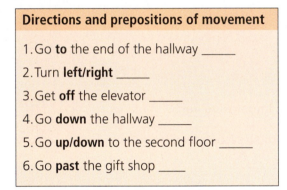

Directions and prepositions of movement

1. Go **to** the end of the hallway _____
2. Turn **left/right** _____
3. Get **off** the elevator _____
4. Go **down** the hallway _____
5. Go **up/down** to the second floor _____
6. Go **past** the gift shop _____

▸ *Grammar Reference page 147*

4 Read the conversations and fill in the blanks.

1. A: Excuse me. Where's the restaurant?
   B: Go _____ to the third floor. Get _____ the elevator. _____ right, go _____ the hallway, and _____ right again. You'll see it on the left. It's Ted's Steakhouse.
   A: Thank you.

2. A: Can I help you?
   B: Is there a fitness center in the hotel?
   A: Yes, ma'am, it's on the fifth floor. Get ____ the elevator, and the fitness center will be in front of you.

3. A: Where's the parking garage?
   B: Go _____ the reception desk and take the elevator. Go _____ to the basement. Get _____ the elevator, and you'll see it right in front of you.

5 🎧 Listen and check your answers.

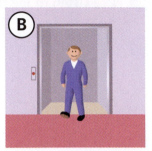

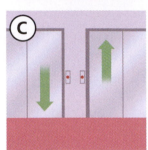

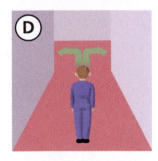

Speaking

6 **PAIRS.** Take turns asking and giving directions in a hotel. You are at the reception desk. Student A, look at page 139. Student B, look at the hotel floor plan below. Ask Student A for directions to these places and label each place on your hotel floor plan.

- fitness center

- gift shop

- business center

- cash machine

B: Where is the finess center?

A: Go down the hallway to the . . .

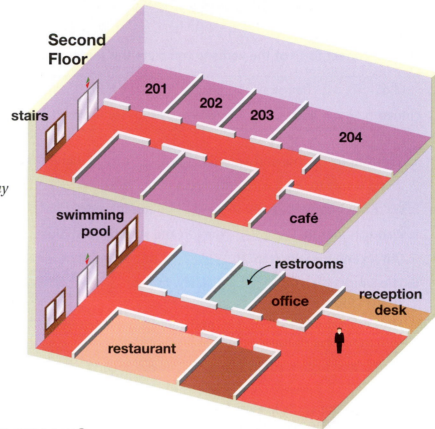

Second Floor

stairs

201

202

203

204

swimming pool

café

restrooms

office

reception desk

restaurant

7 Are your floor plans the same now?

Writing

8 Choose two places in your school. Write directions to get to each place from your classroom. Use imperative forms and expressions for direction.

CONVERSATION TO GO

A: Excuse me, where's the restaurant?
B: **Go to** the tenth floor. **Turn right.** It's **on the left**.

Big plans

Vocabulary Life changes
Grammar *be going to* for future
Speaking Talking about plans

Lesson A

Getting started

1 Use the correct form of the verbs to complete the sentences.

build	change	~~earn~~	escape
move	quit	retire	settle down

1. At the moment, José and Antonio _earn_ a lot of money as computer consultants.

2. Metta wants to _____ the stress of the city.

3. We're not happy. We want to _____ our lifestyle.

4. Wendy hopes to _____ her job and start her own business.

5. Daniel and his wife want to _____ out of the city.

6. The Smiths plan to _____ a new house in the country.

7. They need time to _____ and get comfortable with their new routine.

8. Martin and Josie want to _____ at age 65.

2 *PAIRS.* Use the verbs in Exercise 1 to tell your partner five things you want to do in your life.

Simon and Emily Wilkinson, Atlanta, Georgia.

Reading

3 *PAIRS.* **What does *to have it all* mean? Give examples.**

4 **Read the article about Simon and Emily. Write the details about their life in the city and in the country.**

Life in the city	Life in the country
successful jobs as computer consultants	no electricity

5 **Read the article again and answer these questions.**

Why did Emily and Simon decide to change their lifestyle?
What do you think of their new lifestyle?

Stress-free

BE SUCCESSFUL, MAKE A LOT OF MONEY, and live in a beautiful apartment in the city. Be happy because you "have it all." Many of us dream of these things, but for Emily and Simon Wilkinson of Atlanta, Georgia, it wasn't enough. They had everything, but they weren't happy with their jobs or with life in the city. They wanted to change their lifestyle.

When their friends asked how, they said, "We're going to quit our jobs as computer consultants. We're going to leave our apartment and buy some land in the Cumberland Mountains."

Now, three months later, life is very different. There's no electricity, no shower, and no supermarket nearby to buy food. But the husband and wife team love it, and they have big plans.

So what are they going to do? "First, we're going to build a house. Then we're going to plant a garden so we can have lots of vegetables to eat all year. We're going to settle down in our new life."

And are they going to work in the future? "We're going to offer vacations to business people who need to escape the stress of the city. But this time we aren't going to get stressed because of our jobs! We're going to work in our garden and just relax. We're probably not going to retire when we're 65!"

Grammar focus

1 Study the examples of *be going to* + verb for the future.

> I**'m going to quit** my job.
> We**'re going to build** a house.
> He**'s not going to live** in the city.
> We **aren't going to retire** at age 65.
> Where **are** they **going to go**?
> **Are** you **going to change** your lifestyle? Yes, I **am**. / No, I**'m** not.

2 Look at the examples again. Complete the rule in the chart.

> **be going to for future**
>
> Use a form of the verb _____ + *going to* + the base form of the
> verb to talk about future plans.

Grammar Reference page 148

3 Charlie, Bonnie, and Steffi are Emily and Simon's friends. They plan
to change their lifestyles, too. Write sentences about their plans.

1. What / do? *What are they going to do?*
2. What / their life / be like?
3. Charlie and Bonnie / buy some land in the country
4. They / build a house
5. They / not have / electricity or showers
6. Steffi / leave her apartment / buy a house
7. She / quit her job
8. She / not work in an office
9. She / work from home
10. She / plant a garden

Pronunciation

4 🎧 *Going to* for the future has two pronunciations. Listen to the first
pronunciation. Notice the weak form of *to*.

going to	going to do	What are you going to do?
going to leave	going to leave the city	I'm going to leave the city

5 🎧 Listen to the second pronunciation of *going to*. Notice that there is
no /t/ sound. People often use this pronunciation (*gonna*) in conversation.

6 🎧 Listen and repeat.

Speaking

7 **BEFORE YOU SPEAK.** What are your plans for the future? Check (✓) the things that are true for you. Then write two more things you plan to do.

Next week	In the next six months	In the next three years
get a haircut	move to another city	travel abroad
play soccer	go on vacation	get married
go to work	change my job	earn my degree
go out for dinner	buy new clothes	learn something new
_____	_____	_____
_____	_____	_____

8 **GROUPS OF 3.** Take turns asking each other about your future plans.

A: *What are you going to do next week?*
B: *I'm going to get a haircut.*
C: *Well, I'm going to go out for dinner!*

9 What's the most interesting thing you found out about your partners' plans?

Writing

10 Write a paragraph describing things you're going to do within the next few years. Use *be going to* for future.

CONVERSATION TO GO

A: **Are** you **going to have** children?
B: No, I'**m** not!

Lesson A

A new year

Vocabulary Dates, months, time, ordinal numbers 11th–31st
Grammar Prepositional phrases with time
Speaking Talking about memorable times

Millennium bug!
B

Getting started

1 *PAIRS.* Fill in the blanks on the calendar.

A

2 🎧 Listen and check your answers. Then listen again and repeat.

3 *PAIRS.* Discuss. What's your favorite month? Why? What month is your birthday in?

January								February																					
				1	2	3		1	2	3	4	5	6	7		1	2	3	4	5	6						1	2	3
4	5	6	7	8	9	10		8	9	10	11	12	13	14		7	8	9	10	11	12	13		4	5	6	7	8	9	10
11	12	13	14	15	16	17		15	16	17	18	19	20	21		14	15	16	17	18	19	20		11	12	13	14	15	16	17
18	19	20	21	22	23	24		22	23	24	25	26	27	28		21	22	23	24	25	26	27		18	19	20	21	22	23	24
25	26	27	28	29	30	31		29								28	29	30	31					25	26	27	28	29	30

					1		1	2	3	4	5				1	2	3		1	2	3	4	5	6	7
2	3	4	5	6	7	8	6	7	8	9	10	11	12	4	5	6	7	8	9	10	8	9	10	11	12	13	14
9	10	11	12	13	14	15	13	14	15	16	17	18	19	11	12	13	14	15	16	17	15	16	17	18	19	20	21
16	17	18	19	20	21	22	20	21	22	23	24	25	26	18	19	20	21	22	23	24	22	23	24	25	26	27	28
23	24	25	26	27	28	29	27	28	29	30				25	26	27	28	29	30	31	29	30	31				
30	31																										

		1	2	3	4					1	2		1	2	3	4	5	6				1	2	3	4
5	6	7	8	9	10	11	3	4	5	6	7	8	9	7	8	9	10	11	12	13	5	6	7	8	9	10	11
12	13	14	15	16	17	18	10	11	12	13	14	15	16	14	15	16	17	18	19	20	12	13	14	15	16	17	18
19	20	21	22	23	24	25	17	18	19	20	21	22	23	21	22	23	24	25	26	27	19	20	21	22	23	24	25
26	27	28	29	30			24	25	26	27	28	29	30	28	29	30					26	27	28	29	30	31
							31																			

C

Listening

4 **PAIRS.** **Look at the pictures of important events in 1999. Match the pictures with these events.**

New Year's celebration _____

the solar eclipse _____

the millennium bug scare _____

5 🎧 **Listen to the radio show about 1999 and complete the chart.**

Who?	Where?	What?	When?
Young-Chul	Sydney		
Adriana		the solar eclipse	
Lucas			November and December

Grammar focus

1 Study the examples of time expressions with *at*, *on*, and *in*.

> I tried to see the eclipse **on** Wednesday **at** 11:00 **in** the morning.
> We went to a big party **on** December 31st.
> **In** November and December, I spent most of my time working on programs.

2 Look at the examples again. Complete the chart with *at*, *on*, and *in*.

_____	_____	_____
November (months)	August 11th (dates)	10:00 (times)
1999 (years)	Monday (days)	
the evening (parts of the day)	New Year's Day (holidays)	lunch (mealtimes)
	the weekend	

> **Grammar Reference page 148**

3 Complete the sentences with *at*, *on*, or *in*.

1. What happened __in__ 1999?

2. My daughter was born _____ 6:00 _____ January 1st.

3. What did you do _____ December 31st?

4. I went to a party _____ the evening. It was incredible.

5. I got married _____ February 14th, St. Valentine's Day.

6. I started my new job _____ Monday, October 21st.

7. I went on vacation _____ August.

8. We moved into our new home _____ 2001.

Pronunciation

4 🎧 Listen. Notice the pronunciation of the voiceless *th* sound, /θ/. Then listen again and repeat.

thousand   **th**ird   **th**ink   **th**ree

thirty-first   ten**th**   **th**irtie**th**   **th**irteen**th**

5 *PAIRS.* Say the dates you see on the right.

6 🎧 Listen and and check your answers.
Then listen again and repeat.

Speaking

7 **BEFORE YOU SPEAK.** Think of three important events in your life during the past year. Make notes.

A year in the life of _____	
Date	**Event**

8 **PAIRS.** Take turns telling each other about the important events in your life last year. Ask follow-up questions.

A: *I bought a new car in June. I think it was on June 15th.*
B: *Really? That's great. What kind of car?*

9 **GROUPS OF 4.** Tell the group what your partner did and when. Who had similar experiences?

Writing

10 Think about your life last year. Write a summary of the important events. Use prepositional phrases with time.

CONVERSATION TO GO

A: **When** did you meet your wife?
B: **At** exactly 9:15 **in the evening, on** Monday, August 21, 2000.

Unit 21 Life and times

1 🎧 Listen to the model conversation.

2 Complete the questions with *Who, What, Where, When,* or *Did.*

1. _Did_ you make a lot of changes in your life last year? (yes/no)
2. _____ did you change? (give details)
3. _____ did you spend a lot of time as a child? (place)
4. _____ did you buy the last time you went shopping? (item)
5. _____ did you get married / start school / start your new job? (date)
6. _____ you go on vacation this year? (yes/no)
7. _____ did you go? (location)
8. _____ you see anyone famous on the street, in a restaurant, at a party? (yes/no)
9. _____ did you see? (famous person's person)

3 *PAIRS.* Take turns asking each other questions. Take notes about your partner's information.

4 Which information is the same for you and your partner?

Unit 22 It's on the right.

5 🎧 Listen to the model conversation and look at the floor plan.

6 *GROUPS OF 3.* Students A and B, you are guests at a hotel. Student C, you work at the reception desk. Give directions to different places on the floor plan. Students A and B, take turns guessing each place. The person with the most correct answers wins.

Unit 23 Big plans

7 🎧 Listen to the model conversation.

8 *GROUPS OF 3.* You are going to retire next year! Take turns telling each other what you are going to do with your free time.

9 Now that you've heard what others are planning to do, do you want to change any of your plans? Which ones?

Unit 24 A new year

10 Think about important events in your life in the past year. When did they happen? You have two minutes. Write five events on a piece of paper and turn your paper over.

11 🎧 Listen to the model conversation and look at the chart.

Month		Day					
January	July	1st	2nd	3rd	4th	5th	6th
February	August	7th	8th	9th	10th	11th	12th
March	September	13th	14th	15th	16th	17th	18th
April	October	19th	20th	21st	22nd	23rd	24th
May	November	26th	27th	28th	29th	30th	31st
June	December						

12 *GROUPS OF 4.* Take turns. You have five seconds. Say an event and the date it happened.

13 Change groups. Play again

115

Be my guest.

Vocabulary Verbs related to asking and responding
Grammar Modals: *can* and *could* for permission and requests
Speaking Asking for things and responding

Getting started

1 Underline the correct verb to complete each phrase.

1. <u>call</u> / **ask** a taxi
2. **use** / **take** the phone
3. **pay** / **take** with a check
4. **say** / **tell** someone something
5. **pay** / **sell** by check
6. **call** / **borrow** a friend's car
7. **pay** / **accept** credit cards
8. **tell** / **recommend** a good restaurant
9. **pass** / **give** the sugar

2 *PAIRS.* Compare your answers.

3 *PAIRS.* Make sentences with each phrase. You can use any verb tense.

I always call a taxi when I'm downtown.

TAKE THE QUIZ!

1 **You want to use your friend's phone. What do you say?**
A. Can I use your phone?
B. Where's the phone?

2 **You can't hear what your friend says on the phone. What do you say?**
A. Say that again.
B. Could you say that again?

3 **You want a taxi. What do you say to the hotel doorman?**
A. I want a taxi.
B. Could you call a taxi, please?

4 **The taxi is there, but you're waiting for your friend. What do you say to the taxi driver?**
A. Just a moment.
B. Could you wait just a moment?

Reading

4 **Look at each picture in the quiz and discuss these questions.**

What do you think the people are saying?
Are you usually polite in these situations?
Are there any situations when you are not polite?

How Polite Are You?
Take our quiz and find out how polite you are.

5 You are a hotel clerk. A customer asks, "Can I pay by check?" What do you say?
A. No.
B. I'm sorry. We only accept cash and credit cards.

6 You ask a business client to recommend a good restaurant. What do you say?
A. Tell me about a good restaurant.
B. Could you recommend a good restaurant?

7 You're having dinner with friends and you want some salt. What do you say?
A. Could you pass the salt, please?
B. Salt, please.

8 You want some water with your dinner. What do you say to the waiter?
A. Can I have some water, please?
B. Give me some water.

5 **Take the quiz.**

6 *PAIRS.* **Compare your answers and score your quizzes. Which words do people use in English to make requests more polite?**

Answers

Score one point for each correct answer.

1. a, 2. b, 3. b, 4. b, 5. b,
6. b, 7. a, 8. a

1–3 = not polite
4–6 = polite
7–8 = very polite

Grammar focus

1 Study the examples. Notice the ways to ask permission and make requests, and notice the responses.

> A: **Could I borrow** your phone?
> B: **Sure.**
>
> A: **Can I pay** by check?
> B: **I'm sorry.** We don't accept checks.
>
> A: **Could you pass** the butter, please?
> B: **Of course.**
>
> A: **Can you recommend** a good restaurant?
> B: **Sure.**

2 Look at the examples again. Complete the chart.

Modals: *can* and *could* for permission and requests
Use _____ or _____ + the base form of the verb to ask for permission·
Use _____ or _____ + *you* + the base form of the verb to ask someone to do something or make a request.
Use _____ or _____ to answer *yes*.
Use _____ and give the reason to answer *no*.

> *Grammar Reference page 148*

3 Rewrite the sentences using *Could I/Can I ...?* or *Could you/Can you ...?* to make polite requests. There may be more than one correct answer.

1. I want to borrow your car. *Could I borrow your car?*
2. Pass the bread.
3. Give me your pen to use!
4. I want to pay and I only have a credit card!
5. Spell that again!
6. Recommend a good restaurant.
7. I want to use your cell phone.
8. Give me a cup of coffee!
9. Tell me the way to the Tower Hotel.

Pronunciation

4 🎧 **Listen. Notice the way the voice goes down and then up in these polite requests.**

Could I use your pen, please?

Can I have some water?

Could you call a taxi, please?

Could you pass the butter, please?

Can I pay by check?

Can you recommend a good restaurant?

5 🎧 **Listen again and repeat.**

Speaking

6 *BEFORE YOU SPEAK.* **You are going to ask a partner to do some things. Student A, look at page 139. Student B, look at this page and fill in the blanks.**

- recommend a good _____
- use his/her _____
- borrow his/her _____

- help you with _____
- call a _____ for you

7 *PAIRS.* **Take turns making requests and asking for permission. You can say *yes* only three times. Student B, you start.**

B: *Can you recommend a good restaurant?*
A: *Sure. The Palm Café is one of my fovorites.*

Writing

8 **Write short notes for the following situations.**

1. You need a friend or family member to do something for you, but they are not home so you need to write a note. Make your request and include the reason.

2. You need to borrow something from your neighbors, but they are not home so you need to write a note. Ask for permission and include the reason.

CONVERSATION TO GO

A: **Could I pay** by credit card?
B: **I'm sorry.** We only accept cash.

Lesson A

North and south

Vocabulary Adjectives to describe a country
Grammar Comparative adjectives
Speaking Comparing places

Getting started

1 *PAIRS.* Look at the photos of New Zealand's North Island and South Island. Name some of the things you see.

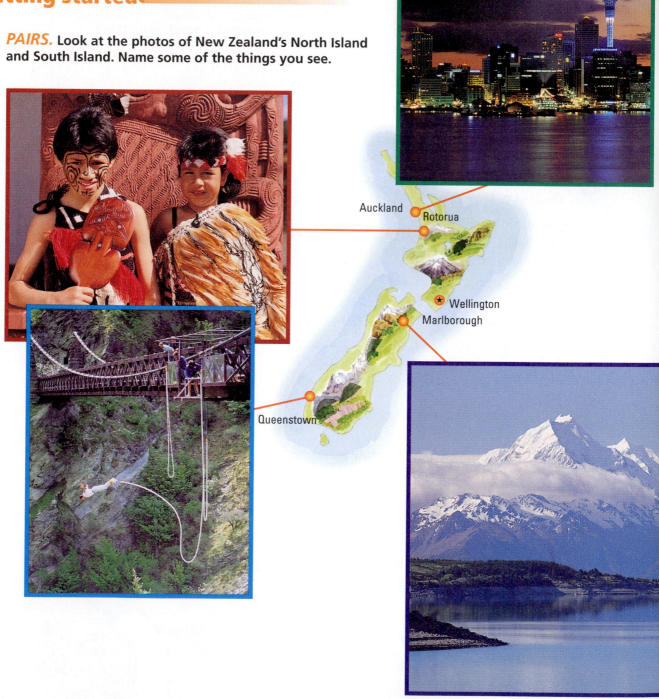

Auckland
Rotorua

Wellington
Marlborough

Queenstown

2 Underline the adjective that does not go with the noun.

1. People: friendly / interesting / <u>empty</u> / unfriendly

2. Cities: cosmopolitan / exciting / historic / delicious / busy

3. Weather: hot / dirty / dry / wet / cold

4. Beaches: clean / dirty / crowded / empty / modern

5. Countryside: flat / small / quiet / beautiful / mountainous

3 *PAIRS.* **Look at the pictures of New Zealand again. Describe the pictures using adjectives from Exercise 2.**

The children from Rotorua have interesting clothes.

Listening

4 🎧 **Listen to three people talk about places in New Zealand. On which island is the place each person talks about, the North Island or the South Island? Write *N* or *S*.**

Speaker 1 ___

Speaker 2 ___

Speaker 3 ___

5 🎧 **Listen again and draw lines to match the places with the descriptions.**

1. Auckland   dry, home of white wine, mountainous

2. Marlborough   crowded, shops open seven days a week

3. Queenstown   modern, big, close to cultural and historic places

Grammar focus

1 **Study the examples of comparative adjectives.**

People are **friendlier** there.	It's **more exciting than** other places in New Zealand.
The climate is **drier**.	The South Island is **more mountainous than** the North Island.

2 **Look at the examples again. Complete the chart.**

Comparative adjectives		
Use the comparative to express a similiarity between two people, places, and things. Use the word _____ when you say both things you are comparing.		
	Adjective	**Comparative**
1 syllable	nice / clean	nicer than / _____ than
Ends in 1 vowel + 1 consonant	big / flat	bigger than / _____ than
Ends in *y*	dry / friendly	drier than / _____ than
2 or more syllables	modern / exciting	_____ than / _____ than
Irregular	good / bad	_____ than / worse than

Grammar Reference page 149

3 **Use the information to write complete sentences comparing the places.**

1. The south of Italy/ hot /the north
   The south of Italy is hotter than the north.
2. Chicago / expensive / Denver
3. The south of France / dry / the north
4. The north of Italy / wet / the south
5. The north of Russia / cold / the south
6. Holland / flat / Germany
7. Tokyo / exciting / Nagoy

Pronunciation

4 🎧 **Listen. Notice the stressed words and the weak pronunciation of *than*.**

bigger	**big**ger **than** New **York**	**Dal**las is **big**ger **than** New **York**.
hotter	**hot**ter **than** the **north**	The **south** is **hot**ter **than** the **north**.
more **mod**ern	more **mod**ern **than Ri**o	Bra**si**lia is more **mod**ern **than Ri**o.
friendlier	**friend**lier **than oth**er **cit**ies	It's **friend**lier **than oth**er **cit**ies.

5 🎧 **Listen and repeat.**

Speaking

6 *PAIRS.* **Choose two cities that you both know well. Write adjectives in the columns to describe each city.**

DESCRIBE THE . . .	CITY #1 _____	CITY #2 _____
People		
Geography		
Restaurants		
Shopping		
Free-time activities		
Weather		
Historical places		

7 *PAIRS.* **Talk about which city is "better." Use the adjectives in the chart to compare them. Come to an agreement.**

A: *I think Miami is better than New Orleans. Miami has better shopping.*
B: *But New Orleans has better restaurants!*
C: *I agree but, . . .*

Writing

8 **Imagine you're going to move to another city (in your country or in another country). Write a paragraph comparing the new city with the place where you live now.**

CONVERSATION TO GO

A: Why do you think the north is **better than** the south?
B: Because I live there!

The best food in town

Vocabulary Adjectives to describe restaurants
Grammar Superlative adjectives
Speaking Describing restaurants

Lesson A

Jumbo

busy

McDonald's

busy

Solo per Due

comfortable

Getting started

1 Describe the restaurants. Write the adjectives in the boxes on the photos.
You will use some words more than one time.

affordable	comfortable	friendly	quiet
big	cute	old	romantic
busy	expensive	popular	slow
cheap	famous	quick	small

2 *PAIRS.* Compare your answers.

Pronunciation

3 **PAIRS.** Write the adjectives from Exercise 1 in the correct column, according to the number of syllables and the stress.

○	○ ○	○ ○ ○	○ ○ ○	○ ○ ○
big cheap cute	busy			

4 🎧 Listen and check your answers. Then listen again and repeat.

Reading

5 Read the reviews of the three restaurants. Then write the names of the restaurant for each review.

This place in Pushkin Square, Moscow, is the busiest and most popular fast-food restaurant in the world. It's part of a chain of 57 restaurants in Russia that serves around 150,000 customers a day. They don't have the cheapest prices, but they do have the quickest service.

1. _____

This is the smallest restaurant in the world. It has only one table and serves only two people at a time. People have come from all over the world to this 19th century villa to sit in front of the fire and enjoy the friendliest service, and the best local food and wine. It probably has the most romantic atmosphere of any restaurant in Italy — maybe even in the world!

2. _____

It is the biggest and the most famous restaurant in Hong Kong. It was built in 1977, and more than 30 million people have eaten at the 4,300 tables on the three boats. The oldest boat is called *Tai Pak*. Some of the most famous guests have included John Wayne and Queen Elizabeth II. You can choose from over 100 different seafood dishes on the menu.

3. _____

6 **PAIRS.** Which restaurant would you like to go to? Why?

27

Grammar focus

1 **Study the examples of superlative adjectives.**

It's **the smallest** restaurant in the world.
The McDonald's in Pushkin Square is **the busiest** fast-food restaurant in the world.
This restaurant probably has **the most romantic** atmosphere of any restaurant in Italy.
It also has **the best** local food and wine.

2 **Look at the examples again. Complete the chart.**

Superlative adjectives		
Use the superlative to compare one person, place, or thing to other people, places, and things. Use the word _____ before the superlative adjective.		
	Adjective	**Superlative**
1 syllable	old / quick	the oldest /_____
Ends in 1 vowel + 1 consonant	big / hot	the biggest /_____
Ends in *y*	noisy / busy	the noisiest /_____
2 or more syllables	famous / romantic	the most famous /_____
Irregular	good / bad	_____ / the worst

Grammar Reference page 149

3 **Complete the conversation with the superlative form of the adjectives in parentheses.**

A: I'm not familiar with the restaurants in town yet.

B: Well, you can ask me. I know them all — <u>the best</u> , _____, and _____.
　　　　　　　　　　　　　　　　　　　　　1. (good)　　　　　2. (bad)　　　　　　　3. (expensive)

A: OK. Is there a good Greek restaurant to go to on a Saturday night?

B: Well, _____ Greek restaurant is Karyatis. The food is great, but it's expensive.
　　　　　4. (famous)

A: What about the new French café downtown?

B: That's definitely _____ place, but it's also _____ place in town.
　　　　　　　　　　5. (romantic)　　　　　　　　　　　6. (small)
　There are only six tables, so it takes a long time to be seated.

A: Ok. Where's _____ restaurant with good food in town?
　　　　　　　　7. (big)

B: Definitely Hua. It's _____ Chinese restaurant in town. It's not
　　　　　　　　　　　8. (popular)

　_____ place, but it definitely has _____ service you
　9. (quiet)　　　　　　　　　　　　　　　　10. (quick)

can find in a big restaurant on a Saturday night. Let's go eat!

4 *PAIRS.* **Practice the conversation in Exercise 3.**

126

Speaking

5 **PAIRS.** Look at the survey. Choose three restaurants you both know in your area and rate them.

A: OK. First, Bella Luna. I think it's affordable. It's definitely not the most expensive.
B: I agree. The food there is really good. I give it a 4. It's not the best.
A: I don't think …

Restaurant Survey

Restaurant name	Bella Luna	_____	_____	_____
Prices				
$=cheap				
$$=affordable	$ $	_____	_____	_____
$$$=expensive				
Other criteria				
1--------------------5 the worst the best				
Food quality	4	_____	_____	_____
Fast service	2	_____	_____	_____
Friendly service	5	_____	_____	_____
Atmosphere	3	_____	_____	_____

6 **PAIRS.** Which restaurant is the best? The worst? Why?

Writing

7 Choose your favorite place to eat. Write a review of the restaurant. Use superlative adjectives and some of the vocabulary in this unit.

CONVERSATION TO GO

A: Where's **the best** place to eat?
B: That restaurant on the corner, but it's also **the most expensive**!

UNIT 28

On the phone

Vocabulary Telephoning
Grammar Present continuous for future
Speaking Taking and leaving messages

Lesson A

Getting started

1 **PAIRS. Match the words in the box with the pictures.**

answering machine ___
area code ___
cell phone _A_
pager ___
text message ___

2 **Complete the sentences with the words and phrases in the box.**

call you back   Directory Assistance
take a message   page
put you on hold   leave a message

1. I'm sorry. John's out today. Can I _take a message_ ?

2. _____. What city and listing?

3. Can I _____ while I check if Mr. King is in the office today?

4. Sorry, Jane is in a meeting. Do you want to _____?

5. Pam is out on a business call. Do you want me to _____ her?

6. I'm sorry. Kate is busy right now. Can she _____ later?

3 🎧 **Listen and check your answers.**

Phone Etiquette at Home

A

B

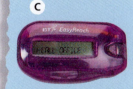
C

D

E
New York 212
San Francisco 415

It's true, most people know how to use the phone. But in today's world, communication skills are essential. In fact, 70% of communication is not what you say, but how you say it.

_____

1. Don't call before 9:00 A.M. or after 9:30 or 10:00 P.M.

2. Say "hello" and give your name. Then ask for the person you want to speak to.

3. When you leave a message, give your name again and your number, if necessary.

4. Thank the other person at the end of the call.

_____

5. The correct way to answer is "hello." Just saying "yes" is considered rude.

6. If the caller asks to speak to a person who is not there, say, "I'm sorry" and offer to take a message.

7. Repeat the caller's message to check that it is correct.

8. Make sure you have the correct number from the caller.

Reading

4 **PAIRS.** Discuss these questions.

Do you like leaving messages on answering machines or voice mail? Why?
Do you prefer using a cell phone or a pager? Why?

5 Read the article on phone etiquette. Write *Answering* or *Calling* in the correct place above sentences 1–4 and 5–8.

6 **PAIRS.** Match the number of the advice from the article with the sentences in the telephone conversation. You can use a number more than once.

A: Hello? _____5_____

B: Hi, this is Tom. Can I speak to Yoko? _____

A: I'm sorry. She isn't here at the moment. Can I take a message? _____

B: Yes, please. Could you tell her I'm not going to class tomorrow night? I'm going away on business. _____

A: OK. You're not going to class. You're going on a business trip. And your name again? _____

B: Tom. My number is 917-555-3487. _____

A: OK. 917-555-3487. I'll ask her to call you. _____

B: Thanks a lot. Bye. _____

Pronunciation

7 🎧 Listen. Notice how a consonant sound at the end of a word links to a vowel sound at the beginning of the next word.

Can I	Can I speak to Yoko?
This is	This is Tom.
She's out at	She's out at the moment.
take a message	Can I take a message?
I'll ask her	I'll ask her to call you.

8 🎧 Listen and repeat.

9 **PAIRS.** Practice the conversation in Exercise 6.

Grammar focus

1 **Study the examples of the present continuous for the future.**

> I'm **leaving** on a business trip after lunch.
> She's **returning** later this morning.
> They're **meeting** in Paris next week.
> We're **giving** a presentation in Rio in a few days.

2 **Look at the examples again. Complete the rule in the chart.**

Present continuous for future
Use the _____ with a future expression marker for a future plan or intention.

Grammar Reference page 149

3 **Read each sentence carefully. Underline the correct form of the verb.**

1. I **am calling** / **call** Miguel tonight.
2. He **is meeting** / **meets** with his friends after work every night.
3. She **is going** / **goes** to the office later this afternoon.
4. Walter **is leaving** / **leaves** on his business trip tonight.
5. They **are having** / **have** these meetings four times a year.
6. He **is buying** / **buys** a new cell phone this weekend.
7. Alessandro always **is taking** / **takes** his laptop to all the meetings.

4 🎧 **Listen to the telephone conversation. Complete the message.**

To: Kang-Hee Moon
Date: June 17
Time: 9:15 A.M.
While you were out

Tom Jones
Business: Building Engineers
Phone: 212-555-4859

Message: _____

Speaking

5 *PAIRS.* Student A, call your friend Pat. Student B, you are Pat's roommate. Pat is not home. Take a message.

> Hello?
> No! Out. Message?
> Number?
> Repeat number?

> Pat/Chris?
> Leaving in afternon / business trip.
> Meet next week. Call me back.
> 212-555-6723
> Yes. Thanks. Goodbye.

6 Role-play. Student B, call your friend, Chris. Student A, you are Chris's roommate. Chris is out of town. Take a message.

Writing

7 🎧 Listen to the two messages on the answering machine. They are for other people in your household. Write the messages.

> Bob—
> Your friend Michele Sakamoto called.
> She . . .

> Lu,
> Victor Chen called. He . . .

CONVERSATION TO GO

A: **Can I speak** to Gustavo, please?
B: **This is** Gustavo.

Unit 25 Be my guest.

1 🎧 Listen to the model conversation. Look at the game.

2 *TWO PAIRS.* Take turns. Toss a coin (one side of the coin = move ahead one space, the other side = move ahead two spaces). When you land on a space, use the cues to make a request. Then ask your partner. Your partner responds to the request. If your request and response are correct, stay on the space. If they are incorrect, move back to where you started your turn. The first pair to reach FINISH wins.

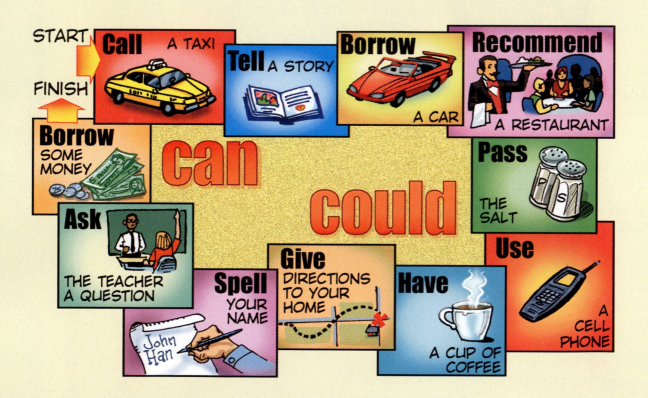

Unit 26 North and south

3 🎧 Listen to the model conversation.

4 *PAIRS.* Think of two cities, towns, or areas in your country. Compare the things that are usually important for quality of life: jobs, schools, geography, people, and free-time activities.

Unit 27 The best food in town

5 🎧 Listen to the model conversation and look at the photo of Jumbo Restaurant.

6 **GROUPS OF 3.** You work for an advertising agency. You're going to create a 30-second commercial for Jumbo Restaurant. Make a list of ideas. Then write a script.

7 Present your commercial to the class. Vote. Which commercial is the funniest? The most creative? The most effective? The most unusual?

Unit 28 On the phone

8 🎧 Listen to the model conversation and look at Message #1.

9 **PAIRS.** Look at each message. Then role-play the conversations.

---

③

Best Communication

To: _Terry Williams_
Date: _June 27_
Time: _2:05 P.M._

While you were out

Pat Chen

Business: _World Group_
Phone: _479-555-5116 ext. 72_

Message: _____ arriving next week
and wants to set up
meetings—call Pat with day
and time you can meet

---

①

First National Bank

To: _Alex Rodriguez_
Date: _June 17_
Time: _9:15 A.M._

While you were out

Chris Perez

Business: _the FAN Group_
Phone: _404-555-3423_

Message: _____ leaving work after
lunch—call Chris back before
_1:00_

---

②

Adrian-

Call Thomas at 972-555-9082.
He's going on vacation tomorrow
and can't bring the dog.
Help!

Dana

World of Music 4

Oh, Pretty Woman
Roy Orbison

Vocabulary

1 *PAIRS.* **Underline the verb to complete each sentence.**

1. You're always so busy. **Walk / <u>Stop</u>** awhile and take a break.

2. Don't go yet. Can't you stay and **talk / say** awhile?

3. You look so sad. Cheer up. Come on, **make / give** me a smile!

4. I can't believe it. There's Jennifer Lopez. Maybe she'll **look / give** my way!

5. Great! You're coming to New York to visit! **Say / Talk** you'll stay with me.

6. Hurry, hurry. A giant sale! Come, **stay / walk** on by. See for yourself.

7. Please be nice to your sister. Don't **give / make** her cry.

8. It's such a great deal. I can't **stay / stop** away – I have to buy it.

9. We're ready to go, but **wait / look**! I can't find the plane tickets.

ROCKABILLY

Rockabilly is a cross between rock and country music. **Roy Orbison** *sang rockabilly in an almost operatic voice. Since his death in 1988, he has been recognized as a true original.*

Listening

2 🎧 **Listen to the song. Which group of sentences matches the story in the song?**

1. The woman walks in the direction of the man.
   The woman walks by the man and stops.
   The woman and the man talk.

2. The woman walks in the direction of the man.
   The woman walks by the man and doesn't stop.
   The woman turns around to walk back to the man.

3. The woman is walking behind the man.
   The woman walks by the man and doesn't stop.
   The woman stops and the man walks by her.

3 🎧 Listen to the song again. Fill in the blanks.

4 *PAIRS.* Check your answers.

Oh, Pretty Woman

Pretty woman walking down the street,

Pretty woman the kind I'd like to _____,

Pretty woman, I don't _____ you,

You're not the truth.

No one could _____ as good as you. Mercy.

Pretty woman, won't you pardon me,

Pretty woman, I couldn't help but _____,

Pretty woman, that you look lovely as can be.

Are you lonely just like me? Pretty woman _____ a while,

Pretty woman _____ a while, pretty woman _____ your smile to me.

Pretty woman yeah, yeah, yeah. Pretty woman _____ my way,

Pretty woman _____ you'll stay with me.

Because I need you, I'll treat you right.

_____ with me baby. _____ mine tonight.

Pretty woman _____ on by. Pretty woman _____ me cry.

Pretty woman _____ away. Hey, OK. If that's the way it must be, OK

I guess I'll _____ on home, it's late

There'll be tomorrow night but _____!

What do I _____? Is she walking back to me?

Yeah, she's walking back to me! Oh, oh, pretty woman.

Speaking

5 *GROUPS OF 3.* Discuss these questions.

Who are the characters in this song? What is the story of their relationship?

Can you create an ending for the story?

a. The pretty woman does turn around and come back and they . . .

b. The pretty woman doesn't come back, so the man . . .

Unit 1, Exercise 7
Student A

Choose three names. Say and spell each one.

A: Jennifer Conklin. J-e-n-n-i-f-e-r C-o-n-k-l-i-n

♀	♂
Jennifer Conklin	Brian Anderson
Lauren Altman	William McMillan
Yuka Hama	Yoshi Hamada
Mei-Fong Chen	Young-Ja Kim
Lorena Marquez	Daniel DaSilva

Unit 3, Exercise 6
Group A

Use the following information to write *Yes/No* questions for a quiz. Use the nationalities on page 10.

Leisure, Sports, and Entertainment

Chess is Indian.

The samba and bossa nova are Brazilian.

Food and Drink

Pita bread and kebabs are Turkish.

Pasta and gelato are Italian.

Famous People

Pelé is Brazilian.

Tiger Woods is American.

Unit 4, Exercises 6 and 7
Students A and B

You need to order office supplies. Call Professional Office Supplies. Order five items. Use the item numbers.

B: Professional Office Supplies. May I help you?
A: Yes, I'd like to order some supplies.
B: OK. What's your last name?

Unit 12, Exercises 5 and 6
Students A and B

Role-play a conversation between a salesperson and a customer. You are the salesperson. Follow the arrows to help create your conversation.

Try to help the customer find and buy what he/she is looking for. Use the items and prices on this page. You can offer items in different colors and sizes.

A: Can I help you?
B: Yes. Do you have this suit in brown?

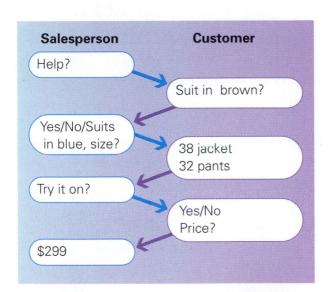

Salesperson	Customer
Help?	
	Suit in brown?
Yes/No/Suits in blue, size?	
	38 jacket 32 pants
Try it on?	
	Yes/No Price?
$299	

$25.00

$75.00

$39.00

$32.00

$20.00

$9.99

$299.00

$35.00

$125.00

Unit 15, Exercise 8
Student A

Look at the picture of the Cormack family. Take turns asking questions to find five differences between your picture and Student B's picture. Take notes.

A: Is the son watching TV?
B: No, he isn't. He's …

In Student B's picture…
_____
_____
_____
_____
_____
_____

Unit 16, Exercise 5
Student A

You are the waiter/waitress. Students B and C will choose what they want from the menu. Take their order.

A: Can I take your order?
B: Yes, I'd like a cheese and tomato sandwich.
C: I'll have a ham sandwich. Can I have a house salad with that, please?

Order #1234

Table

Total

Unit 21, Exercise 6
Student A

Take turns asking and answering questions to complete Marc Anthony's biography.

B: Where did he grow up?
A: He grew up in New York City.

All About
Marc Anthony

His early life

Marc Anthony was born in 1969. His parents were from Puerto Rico, but he grew up in New York City. When he was a child, he loved to sing.

His career

Marc Anthony had his first Spanish hit in the year_____. His popularity started to grow. He sang a song with Jennifer Lopez in 1998. The next year was a big year for Marc Anthony. In 1999, he won a Grammy Award, he made a movie, and he made his _____.

His personal life

But important things happened in 2000 also: That year Marc Anthony made _____. He got married to Dayanara Torres. Marc Anthony and his wife had difficult times in _____. In July they broke up, but six months later they were together again and they had a second wedding ceremony in _____!

Unit 22, Exercises 6 and 7
Student A

Give Student B directions to the places he/she asks for.

B: Where is the finess center?
A: Go down the hallway to the . . .

Ask Student B for directions to these places and label each place on your hotel floor plan.

- café
- swimming pool
- room 204
- restaurant

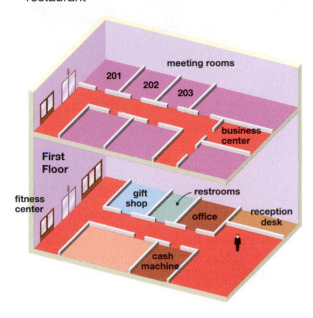

Are your floor plans the same now?

Unit 25, Exercises 6 and 7
Student A

Student A, respond to Student B's questions. You can only say *yes,* three times.

B: Can you recommend a good restaurant?
A: Sure. The Palm Café is one of my favorites.

Now ask Student B the following:

- to recommend a good hotel
- to use his/her computer this weekend
- to borrow his/her car tomorrow
- to make a dinner reservation for tonight
- to pass a dictionary

Unit 1, Exercise 8
Student B

Choose three names. Say and spell each one.

B: Sydney Dowling. S-y-d-n-e-y D-o-w-l-i-n-g

♀	♂
Sydney Dowling	Samuel Rodriguez
Rebecca Ortman	Benjamin Le Febre
Martha Sanchez	Marcos Salles
Akina Abe	Hisa Matsunaga
Ae-Jin Yoon	Min Wang

Unit 3, Exercise 6
Group B

Use the following information to write *Yes/No* questions for a quiz. Use the nationalities on page 10.

Leisure, Sports, and Entertainment

Flamenco is Spanish.

Tai chi is Chinese.

Food and Drink

Sauerkraut is German.

Cognac and champagne are French.

Famous People

Celine Dion is Canadian.

Colin Farrell is Irish.

Review 4, Exercises 7 and 8
Students A and B

Teams take turns. Team 1 goes first. Student C will ask what a Santos family member is doing. Student A, find the person in the picture on this page and pantomime what he or she is doing. Student C will guess using the present continuous tense. Student A, you can only give two pantomime clues.

Then Team 2, take your turn.

Each correct sentence receives one point. Keep score.

Review 4, Exercises 10 and 11
Students A and B

Teams take turns. Team 1 goes first. Look at the menu. Student A, give your order to Student C. Write a (✓) next to the items you order. Ask Student C to repeat your order. Check to see how many items he/she remembers. Subtract a point for each item he/she forgets. Keep score.

Then Team 2, take your turn.

Who remembered the most?

Katie's Good Food Café

Sandwiches:
Chicken (with lettuce) $5.50
Ham (with lettuce) $5.95
Cheese (with lettuce) $4.00

Extras
Tomato $0.50
Mixed green salad $1.75
Potato chips $1.25

Cake
Chocolate $4.50

Fruit
Apple/Banana $1.45

Hot drinks
Tea with lemon Small $1.25 Large $1.80
Coffee Small $1.60 Large $1.95
Hot chocolate Small $1.70 Large $2.00

Cold drinks
Soft drinks Small $1.30 Large $1.50
Orange juice Small $1.30 Large $1.50
Apple juice Small $1.30 Large $1.50
Iced tea Small $1.30 Large $1.50

Review 1, Exercise 9
Student A

You are a game show host. Name an item on this list. The players will try to guess the price. The person who guesses the closest without going over wins the item!

briefcase	$65.00
cell phone	$50.00
desk	$79.00
dictionary	$ 6.75
fax machine	$99.00
file cabinet	$49.00
printer	$89.00
stapler	$ 7.99

Review 5, Exercise 7
Student A

Student A, say a sentence with the time and something that Talia did. Student B, say what Talia didn't do at that time. Then Student B, say a sentence with the time and something Talia didn't do. Student A, say what Talia did do at that time. Take turns saying what Talia did and didn't do.

DAILY PLANNER	
Thursday	**Friday**
8:00 do laundry **X**	8:00 relax and read ✓
9:00 cook breakfast ✓	9:00 try practice test **X**
10:00 finish the newspaper ✓	10:00 Jane arrive? ✓
11:00 ask when Jane arrives **X**	
12:00 organize the party ✓	
5:00 play with the dog ✓	5:00 prepare food ✓
6:00	6:00
7:00 do exercise **X**	7:00 ask Tim for help **X**
8:00	8:00
9:00	9:00 play loud music **X**

Unit 8, Exercise 2
Answer key

Thanksgiving Day
In the U.S.: In November, on the fourth Thursday. Families gather for a traditional meal of turkey, potatoes, gravy, and pie.

In Canada: In October, on the second Monday.

Carnaval
In Brazil, usually in February (sometimes in March). The most famous celebration takes place in Rio de Janeiro. It is always just before the Catholic holy period of Lent, which begins on Ash Wednesday and ends with Easter.

New Year's Day (Shogatsu)
In Japan, on January 1, 2, and 3. People eat special food called *osechi ryori*. The food is packed in a special box and is very colorful (see page 36). People also visit temples and pray for safety, health, and good fortune.

Unit 17, Exercise 6
Answer key

These three places often have hurricanes:

Florida, Jamaica, Mexico

Grammar Reference

Unit 1

be present: singular
- The verb **be** has different forms for the subject pronouns in the present.

I	am	Laura Martin.
It Here That	is	my card.

Long form	Contraction
I **am**	I**'m**
it **is**	it**'s**
here **is**	here**'s**
that **is**	that**'s**

Note: We don't write contractions with most nouns.

My name is Peter.
X My name's Peter.

Unit 2

be simple present; indefinite articles *a/an*

Subject pronouns

Person	Singular	Plural
1st	I	we
2nd	you	you
3rd	he/she/it	they

- Use contractions in conversation and informal writing.

Long Form	Contraction
I **am**	I**'m**
you **are**	you**'re**
he **is**	he**'s**
she **is**	she**'s**
it **is**	it**'s**
we **are**	we**'re**
they **are**	they**'re**

Indefinite articles *a, an*
- Use **a** with singular nouns that begin with a consonant sound.
  a friend
  a roommate
  a university professor
- Use **an** with singular nouns that begin with a vowel sound.
  an artist
  an engineer
  an hourly worker

Unit 3

be present: negative sentences; *Yes/No* questions and short answers

Negative sentences with *be*					
Long form			Contraction		
I	am		I	'm	
You	are		You	're	
He/She/It	is	not British.	He/She/It	's	not Canadian.
We/They	are		We/They	're	

Yes/No questions with *be*			Short answers	
			Affirmative	Negative
Are	you		Yes, I **am**.	No, I**'m not**.
Is	he/she/it	Canadian?	Yes, he/she/it **is**.	No, he/she/it **isn't**.
Are	we/they		Yes, we/they **are**.	No, we/they **aren't**.

Notes:
- Some verbs can be contracted two ways.
  you/we/they **aren't**   =   you/we/they **'re not**
  he/she/it **isn't**   =   he/she/it **'s not**
- Do not use contractions in affirmative short answers.
  A: **Is he** British?
  B: *Yes, **he is**.*
     X Yes, he's.

142

Unit 4

Plurals; *be* present: *Wh*– questions

Plural nouns

- Add **–s** to make most nouns plural.

a wallet	→	*two wallets*
a desk	→	*four desks*
a cell phone	→	*three cell phones*

- Add **–es** to nouns that end in **–ch**, **–sh**, **–s**, or **–x**.

a watch	→	*five watches*
a dish	→	*two dishes*
a glass	→	*three glasses*
a fax	→	*two faxes*

- For nouns that end in consonant + **–y**, change **y** to **i** and add **–es**.

a dictionary	→	*two dictionaries*
a battery	→	*three batteries*

Wh– questions

- Use ***what*** to ask about things.
  What is *your name?*
  What are *your hours?*
- Use ***where*** to ask about places.
  Where is *my pen?*
  Where are *my pens?*
- Use ***how much*** to ask about quantities.
  How much *is a package of paper?*
  How much *are the staples?*

Unit 5

Possessive adjectives and possessive 's

Possessive adjectives	
Subject pronoun	**Possessive adjective**
I	my
you	your
he	his
she	her
it	its
we	our
they	their

Possessive 's

- Use possessive **'s** with singular nouns.
  This is Sarah's favorite song.
  Basketball is David's favorite sport.
  Brazil's vegetables are excellent.
  My dog's favorite food is chicken.

Tom's *His*	*favorite city is Los Angeles.*
Pam's *Her*	*favorite music is salsa.*

- Use an apostrophe (') alone with regular plural nouns.
  The boys' favorite sport is soccer.
  The Corrs' music is excellent.

Note: Use possessive **'s** with irregular plural nouns.
The children's favorite movie is Toy Story.

Unit 6

There is/There are

- Use ***there is / there's*** with a singular noun.
  There is *a hotel.*
  There's *a museum.*
  There isn't *a market.*
  Is there *a Japanese restaurant?*
  Yes, ***there is.*** */ No,* ***there isn't.***
- Use ***there are*** with a plural noun.
  There are *some markets.*
  There aren't *any bookstores.*
  Are there *any schools? Yes,* ***there are.*** */ No,* ***there aren't.***

Note: Use ***any*** with negative statements and questions with ***Are there. . .?***

There isn't any *coffee.*
There aren't any *hotels.*
Are there any *good restaurants?*

Unit 7

Prepositions of location

• Use prepositions of location (**next to**, **above**, **under**, **opposite**, **in front of**, **in**, **on**) to say where things are.
*There's a computer **on** the desk.*
*Is there a ball **under** the table?*
*The stereo isn't **in front of** the window.*

Unit 8

Simple present: affirmative statements

• Use the simple present to talk about routines and habits.

Affirmative		
I/You/We/They	**play**	ball on Sundays.
He/She/It	**plays**	

• Third person (he/she/it):
  Add **–s** to most verbs in the third person singular.
  *He play**s** football everyday.*
  Add **–es** to **do** and **go**, and verbs ending in **–ch**, **–sh**, **–s**, and **–x**.
  *do → does   wash → wash**es***
  *She do**es** her homework.*
  *He wash**es** the dishes.*
  For verbs ending in consonant + **–y**, change **y** to **i** and add **–es**.
  *study → stud**ies***
  *She stud**ies** English.*

Note: The verb **have** is irregular in the simple present.

have → has
*I **have** lunch at 1:00.*
*She **has** breakfast at 8:00.*

Unit 9

Simple present: *Yes/No* questions, short answers, and negative statements

Yes/No questions		
Do	I/you/we/they	collect souvenirs?
Does	he/she/it	

Short answers					
Affirmative			**Negative**		
Yes,	I/you/we/they	**do**.	No,	I/you/we/they	**don't**.
	he/she/it	**does**.		he/she/it	**doesn't**.

Negative statements		
I/You/We/They	**don't**	have a coin collection.
He/She/It	**doesn't**	

Note: The base form of the verb never changes in a question or negative statement.

*Does he **collect** things?*
X Does he collects things?

*He doesn't **collect** things.*
X He doesn't collects things.

Unit 10

Simple present: *Wh–* questions

What When Where Why How	do	I/you/we/they	[base form of the verb]	?
	does	he/she/it		

• Use **what** to ask about things.
  ***What** do you do?*
  ***What** does he do at work?*

- Use *when* to ask about time.
  When do most people usually arrive?
  When does she get to work?
- Use *where* to ask about locations.
  Where do we keep the extra supplies?
  Where does she put the faxes?
- Use *why* to ask about a reason.
  Why do you confirm your reservations?
  Why does the company ask for a number?
- Use *how* to ask about a process.
  How do you usually pay—by cash or credit card?
  How does your boss communicate?

Unit 11

a, an, some, any
- Use *a* or *an* to talk about one thing (singular).
  I take a book and an umbrella.
- Use *some* to talk about more than one thing (plural) when the number is not important.
  We always take some books.
- Use *any* with questions and plural negatives.
  Do you have any credit cards?
  Jack doesn't take any books on vacation.

Note: Use *an* with a singular noun that begins with a vowel sound: *an umbrella*. But *a university* and *a uniform* because these begin with a consonant sound.

Unit 12

Demonstrative adjectives: *this, that, these, those*
- Use *this*, *that*, *these*, and *those* to indicate specific people or things.

	Close	Not close
Singular	this	that
Plural	these	those

This shirt is too plain.
Try it with that jacket over there.
I want to buy these shoes.
Those boots in the corner are nice, too.

Unit 13

Count and non–count nouns; *How much/How many*; Quantifiers: *much, many, a lot of*
- Some nouns are countable. We can count them, and they have plural forms.
  one nut   two nuts
- Other nouns are not countable. We can't count them, and they do not have plural forms.
  meat   X two meats
  ketchup   X three ketchups
- Use *many* with count nouns in questions and negatives.
  There aren't many cookies.
  Does she eat many potato chips?
  How many crackers are on the plate?
- Use *much* with non-count nouns in questions and negatives.
  We don't have much milk.
  Do you drink much juice?
  How much soda is on the table?
- Use *a lot of* with count and non-count nouns in affirmative sentences.
  There's a lot of food.
  There are a lot of apples.

Unit 14

Can for ability
- Use *can/can't* to talk about abilities.

Affirmative	subject + *can* + base form of the verb *We can communicate easily.*
Negative	subject + *can't* + base form of the verb *He can't drive a truck.*
Question	*Can* + subject + base form of the verb *Can you organize information?*
Short answers	Yes + subject + *can* *Yes, I can.*
	No + subject + *can't* *No, I can't.*

Note: *Can/Can't* do not change in the third-person singular.

He can type.
X He cans type.

Unit 15

Present continuous for now

• Use the present continuous to describe what is happening now (at this moment).

Affirmative	subject + **be** + verb + **–ing** I**'m helping** my mom. We**'re talking** to our friends. He**'s cooking** lunch.
Negative	subject + **be** + **not** + verb + **–ing** They **aren't** drinking coffee. He**'s not playing** soccer. We**'re not watching** TV.
Questions	**be** + subject + verb + **–ing** **Are** you **cleaning** the house? **Is** she **getting** up?
Short answers	Yes + subject + **be** Yes, I **am**. Yes, she **is**.
	No + subject + **be** + **not** No, I**'m not**. No, she **isn't**.

• Spelling rules
  - Add **–ing** to most verbs.
    play → playing   visit → visiting
  - For verbs ending in consonant + **–e**, take away **e** and add **–ing**.
    shine → shining   make → making
  - For most one-syllable verbs that end in a consonant + a vowel + a consonant, double the consonant and add **–ing**.
    sit → sitting   get → getting

Unit 16

Modals: *would like, will have,* and *can* for ordering

• Use **would like** (**'d like**) and **will have** to order in a restaurant.
  *I**'d like** a cup of tea, please.*
  *We**'ll have** two chicken sandwiches.*

• Use **can + have** in a *Yes/No* question form to order in a restaurant.
  ***Can I have** a cup of coffee please?*

Unit 17

Action vs. non-action verbs

• Action verbs tell what someone or something does.
• Non-action verbs describe states or situations. They are not normally used in the present continuous.
• Non-action verbs . . .

  describe a state of being.
  *The temperature **is** 75 degrees.*

  show possession.
  *They all **have** umbrellas.*

  describe perceptions.
  *Paris **looks** beautiful in April.*

  describe mental states.
  *They **know** the reason.*

  express likes and dislikes.
  *They **like** the weather there.*

Unit 18

Be simple past

• The verb **be** is irregular in the past.

Affirmative		
I/He/She/It	**was**	there yesterday.
You/We/They	**were**	
Negative		
I/He/She/It	**wasn't**	in class last night.
You/We/They	**weren't**	

Yes/No questions		
Was	I/he/she/it	**ready**?
Were	you/we/they	
Short answers		
Affirmative		**Negative**

Yes,	I/he/she/it **was**.	No,	I/he/she/it **wasn't**.
	you/we/they **were**.		you/we/they **weren't**.

Note: The simple past of **there is/are** is **there was/were**.

Unit 19

Simple past: regular verbs (affirmative and negative)

- Use the simple past to talk about completed actions in the past, often with a time expression, such as **yesterday**, **last Monday**, **two weeks ago**, etc.

  I **called** you last Monday.
  She **studied** in London last year.

- To form the negative of the simple past, use **didn't** + the base form of the verb.

  They **didn't stay**.
  I **didn't talk** to a lot of people.

- Spelling rules:
  - Add **–ed** to most regular verbs.
    talk → talk**ed**
    visit → visit**ed**
    open → open**ed**
  - Add **–d** to verbs that end in consonant + **–e**.
    dance → danc**ed**
    arrive → arriv**ed**
    close → clos**ed**
  - For verbs that end in consonant + **–y**, change **y** to **i** and add **–ed**.
    study → stud**ied**
    try → tr**ied**
    reply → repl**ied**

Unit 20

Simple past: irregular verbs

- Many verbs have irregular simple past forms. Irregular verbs usually do NOT end in **–ed** in the simple past. A list of irregular verbs is on page 150.

  I often **fall** in love.
  I **fell** in love last week.

  He often **buys** flowers.
  He **bought** flowers yesterday.

  We **meet** Sue every Tuesday.
  We **met** Sue last Tuesday.

- The irregular simple past form is ONLY used in affirmative sentences. Negative sentences in the past use **didn't** + the base form of the verb.

  (+) Frank **saw** Mary at the party.
  (–) Frank **didn't see** Gail at the party.

Unit 21

Simple past: questions

Yes/No questions		
Did	I/you	**go**?
	he/she/it	
	we/they	
Short answers		

Affirmative			Negative		
Yes,	I/you	**did**.	No,	I/you	**didn't**.
	he/she/it			he/she/it	
	we/they			we/they	

Wh– questions
Wh– word + **did** + subject + base form of the verb
Who did she talk to? **When** did they leave? **Where** did he live?

Unit 22

Imperatives; directions and prepositional phrases

Imperatives

- Use imperatives to give a command (to tell someone to do something).

Affirmative	base form of the verb **Go** straight. **Turn** left.
Negative	**don't** + base form of the verb **Don't turn** left. **Don't take** the stairs.

Directions and prepositional phrases

- Use the imperative and words such as **up/down**, **left/right**, **off**, **to the end**, **past**, to give directions.
  Drive **past** the parking garage.
  Go **down** to the basement.
  Walk **up** the street.
  Turn **left** on Main Street.

Unit 23

Be going to for future
- Use *be going to* + the base form of the verb to talk about future plans.

Affirmative		
I	am	
You/We/They	are	going to have a party.
He/She/It	is	
Negative		
I	'm not	
You/We/They	aren't	going to have a party.
He/She/It	isn't	

Yes/No questions		
Am	I	
Are	you/we/they	going to have a party?
Is	he/she/it	

Short Answers				
Affirmative		Negative		
Yes,	you/we/they **are**.	No,	you/we/they **aren't**.
	I **am**.		I'm **not**.
	he/she/it **is**.		he/she/it **isn't**.

- You can use **Wh-** words to ask questions about future plans.

Wh– questions
Wh– word + **am/is/are** + subject + **going to** + base form of the verb
What are you going to do?
When are we going to leave?
Where are they going to go?
Why is she going to move?

Unit 24

Prepositional phrases with time
- Use *in* with months, years, and parts of the day.
  *Memorial Day is **in** May.*
  *We met **in** 1973.*
  *The picnic starts **in** the afternoon.*
- Use *on* with days, dates, specific holidays.
  *We're going to a party **on** Friday.*
  *My course starts **on** June 28.*
  *The post office is closed **on** Presidents' Day.*
- Use *at* with specific times, mealtimes, and in the expression *at night*.
  *I'll see you **at** eight o'clock.*
  *They always talk to each other **at** breakfast.*
  *The stars shine brightly **at** night.*

Note: Don't use a preposition with these words: *yesterday, today, tomorrow, last week/month/ year, next week/month/year.*

*They went shopping **last week**.*
*We're going to the beach **tomorrow**.*

Unit 25

Modals: *can* and *could* for permission and requests
- Use *can* or *could* to ask permission to do something.

can/could + subject + base form of the verb
Can I open the window?
I'm sorry. The window doesn't open.
Could we borrow your car?
Yes, of course.

- Use *can* or *could* to make a request.

can or *could* + you + base form of the verb
Can you help me with this, please?
Yes, sure.
Could you call a taxi, please?
Yes, of course.

Unit 26

Comparative adjectives

• Use the comparative form of adjectives with **than** to compare two things or people.

Adjective	Comparative
one syllable warm cold	add **-er** warm**er** than col**der** than
one syllable, ends with vowel + consonant hot big	double the consonant and add **-er** hot**ter** than big**ger** than
two syllables, ends with **y** empty busy	change **y** to **i** and add **-er** empt**ier** than bus**ier** than
two syllables or more historical beautiful	**more** + adjective **more** historical than **more** beautiful than
irregular good bad	**better** than **worse** than

Note: Use the word **than** only when you say both things that you are comparing.

Which is bigger, France or Spain?
France is bigger.
*France is bigger **than** Spain.*

Unit 27

Superlative adjectives

• Use **the** and superlative forms of adjectives to compare three or more things or people.

Adjective	Superlative
one syllable slow clean	add **-est** **the** slow**est** **the** clean**est**
one syllable, ends with vowel + consonant hot big	double the consonant and add **-est** **the** hottest **the** biggest
one syllable, ends with y hungry busy	change **y** to **i** and add **-est** **the** hungr**iest** **the** bus**iest**
two syllables or more expensive famous	**the most** + adjective **the most** expensive **the most** famous
irregular good bad	**the best** **the worst**

*She's **the oldest** woman in the world.*
*It's **the most** expensive hotel in New York.*
***The best** restaurant is Hua.*

Unit 28

Present continuous for future

• You can use the present continuous to talk about future plans.

> **am/is/are** + base form of the verb + **-ing** + future time marker
>
> I **am calling** him back tonight.
> The flight **is leaving** tomorrow morning.
> When **are** you **meeting**?
> We**'re meeting** at 7:00.

Irregular Verbs

Simple present	Simple past	Simple present	Simple past
be	was/were	leave	left
become	became	make	made
begin	began	meet	met
break	broke	put	put
build	built	quit	quit
buy	bought	run	ran
choose	chose	read	read
come	came	say	said
cost	cost	see	saw
do	did	sell	sold
draw	drew	send	sent
drink	drank	sing	sang
drive	drove	sit	sat
eat	ate	sleep	slept
fall	fell	speak	spoke
feel	felt	spend	spent
find	found	swim	swam
fly	flew	take	took
get	got	teach	taught
give	gave	tell	told
go	went	think	thought
grow	grew	understand	understood
have	had	wear	wore
hear	heard	win	won
know	knew	write	wrote

Vocabulary

Unit 1

Hello.
Hi.

Bye.
Goodbye.
See you.
So long.
Thank you.
Thanks.

Excuse me, what's your name again?
Here's my (business) card.
I'm . . .
I'm sorry, could you repeat that?
I'm with . . .
It's nice meeting you.
My name is . . .
Nice to meet you.
Nice to meet you, too.
Pleased to meet you.

Unit 2

architect
artist
assistant
businessman/businesswoman
cashier
doctor
engineer
flight attendant
graphic designer
musician
teacher
waiter/waitress

zero
one
two
three
four
five
six
seven
eight
nine
ten
eleven
twelve
thirteen
fourteen
fifteen
sixteen
seventeen
eighteen
nineteen

Unit 3

Australia/Australian
Argentina/Argentinian
Brazil/Brazilian
Canada/Canadian
China/Chinese
France/French
Germany/German
India/Indian
Japan/Japanese
Korea/Korean
Italy/Italian
Ireland/Irish
Mexico/Mexican
Spain/Spanish
Thailand/Thai
Turkey/Turkish
the United Kingdom/British
the United States /American

Unit 4

battery
briefcase
box of paper clips
cell phone
desk
dictionary
fax machine
file cabinet
folder
notepad
printer
stapler

twenty
thirty
forty
fifty
sixty
seventy
eighty
ninety

Unit 5

baseball game
book
market
magazine
movie
museum
newspaper
restaurant
store
TV show

Unit 6

bad
big
boring
cheap
crowded
delicious
empty
expensive
friendly
good
interesting
small
terrible
unfriendly
wonderful

Unit 7

armchair
bookcase
cabinet
calendar
chair
computer
desk
lamp
plant
printer
sofa
stereo
table
telephone
wastebasket

Unit 8

cook lunch
dance to salsa music
drink juice
eat ice cream
get up at 8:00
give a present
go for a walk
play a game
visit a friend
wash the dishes

Unit 9

book
clock
doll
photo album
picture
plate
postcard
poster
stuffed animal
toy
T-shirt
video

Vocabulary

one hundred
one thousand
ten thousand
one hundred thousand
one million

Unit 10
book a hotel
buy books
contact friends
do your banking
get your news
listen to music
use the Internet

Unit 11
alarm clock
bathing suit
beach towel
books to read
camera
CDs
credit card
film
guidebook
hiking boots
map
phrasebook
portable CD player
sunglasses
sweaters
traveler's checks
umbrella

bicycle
boat
bus
car
motorcycle
plane
subway
taxi
train
trolley

Unit 12
boots
coat
jacket
pants
shirt
shoes
shorts
skirt
sneakers
suit
sweater

T-shirt
extra large
extra small
large
medium
small

Unit 13
beer
bread
butter
cake
candy
cheese
chocolate
coffee
cookies
crackers
fruit
ice cream
nuts
potato chips
soda

Unit 14
design a website
drive a car
manage a hotel
read a story
repair a car
sing a song
speak a language
type a letter
write a report

Unit 15
aunt
brother
child/children
daughter
father
grandfather
grandmother
husband
mother
parents
sister
son
uncle
wife

Unit 16
apple
banana
bottled water
cake
cheese
chicken

chocolate
coffee
drinks
extras
fruit
ham
hot chocolate
juice
lemon
lettuce
milk
mixed green salad
potato chips
sandwich
soft drink
tea
tomato

Unit 17
cold
cool
degrees
hot
hurricane
raining
snowing
sunny
warm
windy

autumn
spring
summer
winter

boots
gloves
hat
jacket
raincoat
sandals
scarf
shorts
sun hat
sweater
T-shirt
umbrella

Unit 18
bicycle

best friend
boyfriend
girlfriend
grandmother

birthday
vacation

Unit 19

arrive
call
close
decide
finish
open
relax
reply
start
watch

Unit 20

be
buy
come
fall (in love)
give
go
know
leave
meet
say
see
think

Unit 21

be born
become famous
get married
go to college
have children
make a film
move to a house
start/finish school
take an English class

Unit 22

business center
café
cash machine
elevator
fitness center
gift shop
hallway
meeting rooms
parking garage
reception desk
restaurant
restrooms
stairs
swimming pool

first
second
third
fourth
fifth

sixth
seventh
eighth
ninth
tenth

Unit 23

build
change
earn
escape
move
quit
retire
settle down

Unit 24

January
February
March
April
May
June
July
August
September
October
November
December

eleventh
twelfth
thirteenth
fourteenth
fifteenth
sixteenth
seventeenth
eighteenth
nineteenth
twentieth
twenty-first
twenty-second
twenty-third
twenty-fourth
twenty-fifth
twenty-sixth
twenty-seventh
twenty-eighth
twenty-ninth
thirtieth
thirty-first

Unit 25

accept checks
borrow something from someone
call a taxi
pass the salt
pay bills

recommend a restaurant
tell someone something
use the phone

Unit 26

beautiful
busy
clean
cold
cosmopolitan
crowded
delicious
dirty
dry
empty
exciting
flat
friendly
historic
hot
interesting
modern
mountainous
quiet
small
unfriendly
wet

Unit 27

affordable
big
busy
cheap
comfortable
cute
expensive
famous
friendly
old
popular
quick
quiet
romantic
slow
small

Unit 28

answering machine
area code
call you back
cell phone
directory assistance
leave a message
page
pager
put you on hold
take a message
text message

Acknowledgments

The authors and series editor wish to acknowledge with gratitude the following reviewers, consultants, and piloters for their thoughtful contributions to the development of *WorldView*.

BRAZIL: São Paulo: Sérgio Gabriel, **FMU/Cultura Inglesa, Jundiaí;** Heloísa Helena Medeiros Ramos, **Kiddy and Teen;** Zaina Nunes, Márcia Mathias Pinto, Angelita Goulvea Quevedo, **Pontifícia Universidade Católica;** Rosa Laquimia Souza, **FMU-FIAM;** Élcio Camilo Alves de Souza, Marie Adele Ryan, **Associação Alumni;** Maria Antonieta Gagliardi, **Centro Británico;** Chris Ritchie, Debora Schisler, Sandra Natalini, **Sevenidiomas;** Joacyr Oliveira, **FMU;** Maria Thereza Garrelhas Gentil, **Colégio Mackenzie;** Carlos Renato Lopes, **Uni-Santana;** Yara M. Bannwart Rago, **Associação Escola Graduada de São Paulo;** Jacqueline Zilberman, **Instituto King's Cross;** Vera Lúcia Cardoso Berk, **Talkative Idioms Center;** Ana Paula Hoepers, **Instituto Winners;** Carlos C.S. de Celis, Daniel Martins Neto, **CEL-LEP;** Maria Carmen Castellani, **União Cultural Brasil Estados Unidos;** Kátia Martins P. de Moraes Leme, **Colégio Pueri Domus;** Luciene Martins Farias, **Aliança Brasil Estados Unidos;** Neide Aparecida Silva, **Cultura Inglesa;** Áurea Shinto, **Santos:** Maria Lúcia Bastos, **Instituto Four Seasons. CANADA:** Stella Waterman, **Camosun College. COLOMBIA: Bogota:** Sergio Monguí, Rafael Díaz Morales, **Universidad de la Salle;** Yecid Ortega Páez, Yojanna Ruiz G., **Universidad Javeriana;** Merry García Metzger, **Universidad Minuto de Dios;** Maria Caterina Barbosa, **Coninglés;** Nelson Martínez R., **Asesorías Académicas;** Eduardo Martínez, Stella Lozano Vega, **Universidad Santo Tomás de Aquino;** Kenneth McIntyre, **ABC English Institute. JAPAN: Tokyo:** Peter Bellars, **Obirin University;** Michael Kenning, **Takushoku University;** Martin Meldrum, **Takushoku University;** Carol Ann Moritz, **New International School;** Mary Sandkamp, **Musashi Sakai;** Dan Thompson, **Yachiyo Chiba-ken/American Language Institute;** Carol Vaughn, **Kanto Kokusai High School. Osaka:** Lance Burrows, **Osaka Prefecture Settsu High School;** Bonnie Carpenter, **Mukogawa Joshi Daigaku/ Hannan Daigaku;** Josh Glaser, Richard Roy, **Human International University/Osaka Jogakuin Junior College;** Gregg Kennerly, **Osaka YMCA;** Ted Ostis, **Otemon University;** Chris Page, **ECC Language Institute;** Leon Pinsky, **Kwansei Gakuin University;** Chris Ruddenklau, **Kinki University;** John Smith, **Osaka International University. Saitama:** Marie Cosgrove, **Surugadai University. Kobe:** Donna Fujimoto, **Kobe University of Commerce. KOREA: Seoul:** Adrienne Edwards-Daugherty, Min Hee Kang, James Kirkmeyer, Paula Reynolds, Warren Weappa, Matthew Williams, **YBM ELS Shinchon;** Brian Cook, Jack Scott, Russell Tandy, **Hanseoung College. MEXICO: Mexico City:** Alberto Hern, **Instituto Anglo Americano de Idiomas;** Eugenia Carbonell, **Universidad Interamericana;** Cecilia Rey Gutiérrez, María del Rosario Escalada Ruiz, **Universidad Motolinia;** Salvador Castañeda, Alan Bond, Eduardo Fernández, Carla Silva, **Universidad Panamericana;** Raquel Márquez Colin, **Universidad St. John's;** Francisco Castillo, Carlos René Malacara Ramos, **CELE – UNAM/Mascarones;** Belem Saint Martin, **Preparatoria ISEC;** María Guadalupe Aguirre Hernández, **Comunidad Educativa Montessori;** Isel Vargas Ruelas, Patricia Contreras, **Centro Universitario Oparin;** Gabriela Juárez Hernández, Arturo Vergara Esteban Juan, **English Fast Center;** Jesús Armando Martínez Salgado, **Preparatoria Leon Tolstoi;** Regina Peña Martínez, **Centro Escolar Anahuac;** Guadalupe Buenrostro, **Colegio Partenon;** Rosendo Rivera Sánchez, **Colegio Anglo Español;** María Rosario Hernández Reyes, **Escuela Preparatoria Monte Albán;** Fernanda Cruzado, **Instituto Tecnológico del Sur;** Janet Harris M., **Colegio Anglo Español;** Rosalba Pérez Contreras, **Centro Lingüístico Empresarial. Ecatepec:** Diana Patricia Ordaz García, **Comunidad Educativa Montessori;** Leticia Ricart P., **Colegio Holandés;** Samuel Hernández B., **Instituto Cultural Renacimiento. Tlalpan:** Ana María Cortés, **Centro Educativo José P. Cacho. San Luis Potosí:** Sigi Orta Hernández, María de Guadalupe Barrientos J., **Instituto Hispano Inglés;** Antonieta Raya Z., **Instituto Potosino;** Gloria Carpizo, **Seminario Mayor Arquidiocesano de San Luis Potosí;** Susana Prieto Noyola, Silvia Yolanda Ortiz Romo, **Universidad Politécnica de San Luis Potosí;** Rosa Arrendondo Flores, **Instituto Potosino/Universidad Champagnat;** María Cristina Carmillo, María Carmen García Leos, **Departamento Universitario de Inglés, UASLP;** María Gloria Candia Castro, **Universidad Tecnológica SLP;** Bertha Guadalupe Garza Treviño, **Centro de Idiomas, UASLP. Guadalajara:** Nancy Patricia Gómez Ley, **Escuela Técnica Palmares;** Gabriela Michel Vázquez, Jim Nixon, **Colegio Cervantes Costa Rica;** Abraham Barbosa Martínez, Lucía Huerta Cervantes, Paulina Cervantes Fernández, Audrey Lizaola López, **Colegio Enrique de Osso;** Ana Cristina Plascencia Haro, Joaquín Limón Ramos, **Centro Educativo Tlaquepaque III;** Rocío de Miguel, **Colegio La Paz;** Hilda Delgado Parga, **Colegio D'Monaco;** Claudia Rodríguez, **English Key. León:** Laura Montes de la Serna, **Colegio Británico A.C.;** Antoinette Marie Hernández, **"The Place 4U2 Learn" Language School;** Delia Zavala Torres, Verónica Medellín Urbina, **EPCA Sur;** María Eugenia Gutiérrez Mena, Ana Paulina Suárez Cervantes, **Universidad la Salle;** Herlinda Rodríguez Hernández, **Instituto Mundo Verde;** María Rosario Torres Neri, **Instituto Jassa. Aguascalientes:** María Teresa Robles Cázares, **Escuela de la Ciudad de Aguascalientes / Universidad de Aguascalientes;** María Dolores Jiménez Chávez, **ECA – Universidad Autónoma de Aguascalientes;** María Aguirre Hernández, **ECA – Proyecto Start;** Fernando Xavier Gómez Orenday, **UAA – IEA "Keep On";** Felisia Guadalupe García Ruiz, **Universidad Tecnológica;** Margarita Zapiain B., **Universidad Autónoma de Aguascalientes;** Martha Ayala Cardoza, **Universidad de la Concordia / Escuela de la Ciudad de Aguascalientes;** Gloria Aguirre Hernández, **Escuela de la Ciudad de Aguascalientes;** Hector Arturo Moreno Díaz, **Universidad Bonaterra.**